Table of Contents

Dedication

To Emmit, Harper, and Jack: Never stop exploring!

Virgin River Narrows at Zion National Park

Acknowledgments

Thanks to my team at the St. Regis Deer Valley for your local knowledge and tips, as well as for giving me the time I needed to write this book! Also many thanks to Visit Salt Lake for providing me with a Connect Pass to access many of the local Salt Lake City attractions.

Notes:

- No site in this book requires four-wheel-drive access; there are many dirt/gravel roads that I traveled easily in a crossover all-wheel-drive SUV.
- Nearly 70 percent of the population in Utah affiliates with The Church of Jesus Christ of Latter-day Saints, which means a lot of restaurants and attractions are closed on Sundays. Always check ahead if you plan to travel on a Sunday.

Apple pie at Capitol Reef National Park

UTAH MAY NOT HAVE the same culinary cachet as a place such as New York City, but there are certainly some unique culinary experiences to be found here. Michelin stars may be limited to the big-city regions, but Utah certainly has its share of James Beard finalists. From mountaintop dining to food tours, these are a few recommendations and experiences for the foodies visiting Utah.

CULINARY EXPERIENCES

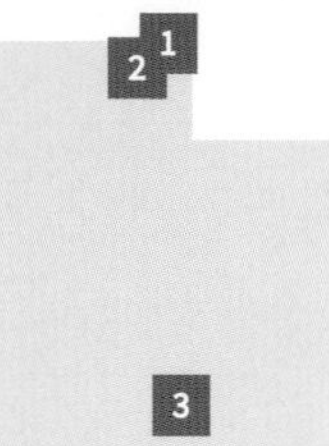

2 Multiple locations

1 Bear Lake Raspberry Shakes

Bear Lake Boulevard, Garden City, UT 84028

Tucked away in the northeast corner of Utah, Bear Lake splits the border of Idaho and Utah. This beautiful lake is known as the "Caribbean of the Rockies," but it is also known as the birthplace of the raspberry shake. In the small town of Garden City on the western shore of the lake, several shake shops vie for the title of "best raspberry shake." Sampling at least one is a must when you visit the area. LaBeau's, Zips, and Quick-and-Tasty are just a few of the contenders for the best raspberry shake in Bear Lake.

Bear Lake's famous raspberry shakes from La Beau's

2 Cache Valley Foodie Trek

Multiple locations near Logan, UT
explorelogan.com/food-tour.html

This self-guided tour takes you through Cache Valley, a lush oasis in the arid state of Utah. Thanks to abundant rivers and streams, plus innovative irrigation systems, Cache Valley is rich in agriculture. Many artisan foods are produced locally and showcased on this tour. Drive US Highway 89 between Willard and Perry, and you'll see dozens of roadside fruit stands peddling local fruits and vegetables, giving this stretch of road the name of "Fruit Way." Other highlights of the Foodie Trek include:

- **Aggie Ice Cream and True Blue Cheese** is part of Utah State University's College of Agriculture and produces some of the best ice cream and cheese in the West.
- **The Beehive Pub & Grill on Logan's Main Street** brews root beer on-site and makes its own gelato.
- **Bluebird Candy Company** has been crafting hand-dipped chocolates in Logan since 1914.
- **Cox Honeyland and Gifts** features locally made honey products from Utah honeybees; they also have a hive that you can observe at the gift shop.

3 Fruita Orchards

Capitol Reef National Park, Fruita, UT
nps.gov/care/learn/historyculture/orchards.htm

The Fruita Orchards in Capitol Reef National Park are listed on the National Register of Historic Places and are the largest collection of historic orchards in the National Park System. Latter-day Saints pioneers planted thousands of fruit trees in the land along the Fremont River. The park maintains the orchards today, using heritage techniques. Flowering trees kick off the season in spring, with harvests beginning in the summer and stretching into fall. The orchards are open to the public for picking, with self-pay stations and scales at the entrance to each orchard. Don't miss out on the fresh-baked pie at the Gifford Homestead, a historic home located at the center of the orchards. They serve tasty pies made with whatever is in season.

4, 5, 7

6

6 Multiple locations

4 Local Food Walking Tours

Salt Lake City and Park City, UT; 801-597-1157
localfoodwalkingtours.com

Food tours are a great way to sample local cuisine and learn about the region you are visiting. Food tour guide Maurice "Moe" Egan hand-picks local restaurants across a variety of cuisines where guests can sample a dish before moving on to the next stop. In order to allow you time to digest between stops, you'll stop at other points of interest along the way. For example, in Park City, there's an art gallery hiding a nineteenth-century bank vault and relics from old mines of the area. Think of it as a progressive dinner with a side of history!

5 Snowed Inn Sleigh Rides

1310 Lowell Avenue, Park City, UT 84060; 435-647-3310
snowedinnsleigh.com

A fun dinner experience on the slopes of Park City Mountain Resort. Start your evening with a sleigh ride pulled by two draft horses that will deliver you to the Snowed Inn Lodge. You can reserve just the sleigh ride, but once you see the lodge, you'll want to stay for dinner! The lodge features a three-course gourmet cowboy dinner, complete with live entertainment. For one fixed price, you get a sleigh experience, dinner, and a show! At the end of the evening, your horse-drawn sleigh will return you to the base of Park City Mountain Resort.

6 The Sweet Tour

Multiple locations in Parowan, UT
thesweettour.com

Parowan is a small town nestled between Beaver and Cedar City and is often overlooked when it comes to tourism. Thus, they decided to brand themselves as the home of "the best cinnamon roll in the West" and challenged several local businesses to throw their hats in the ring. Take a break from your southern Utah road trip and stop by Main Street to grab a few cinnamon rolls. Calvario's, Parowan Cafe, and the local Chevron and Maverick gas stations are just a few bakeries where you can grab a cinnamon roll in Parowan.

7 The Viking Yurt

1345 Lowell Avenue, Park City, UT 84060; 435-615-9878
thevikingyurt.com

This magical dining experience begins at the base of Park City Mountain Resort, where you'll hop aboard a sleigh pulled by a snowcat. Ascending the ski slopes for 23 minutes and 1,800 vertical feet, you'll arrive at the Viking Yurt. You can also choose to ride inside the heated cab of the snowcat. Inside the yurt, you'll be treated to live music courtesy of a baby grand piano. Enjoy a six-course prix fixe Norwegian-style menu, with beer, wine, and liquor available for purchase. Make reservations early as this is a popular Park City dining event.

Viking Yurt, Park City Mountain Resort

Stargazing (star trail image above) is especially popular at Bryce Canyon; an annual astronomy festival is held there each June.

UTAH HOSTED THE BIGGEST festival of all during the 2002 Winter Olympics, so it's safe to say Utahns know how to throw a party! From quaint small-town fêtes to Hollywood-produced film festivals, there's always something fun going on in Utah.

FESTIVALS

Park City, where the Sundance Film Festival is held each year.

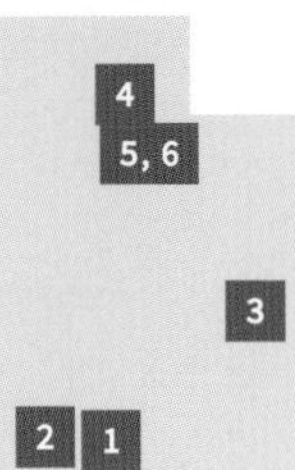

1 Annual Astronomy Festival

Mid-June
Bryce Canyon National Park, UT; 435-834-5322
nps.gov/brca/planyourvisit/astrofest.htm

As one of Utah's Dark Sky Parks, Bryce Canyon National Park celebrates the dark night skies and lack of light pollution with the Annual Astronomy Festival. For more than 20 years, rangers at Bryce Canyon have been offering astronomy programs. Currently offered for four days in June at the time of the new moon, the festival includes family-friendly daytime activities and evening programs. Telescope and constellation tours are offered alongside ranger-led talks, including a keynote topic held at nearby Ebenezer's Barn and Grill.

2 Cedar City Livestock & Heritage Festival

Late October
Cross Hollow Event Center, 11 N Cross Hollow Road, Cedar City, UT 84720; 435-586-8132
cedarlivestockfest.com

Southern Utah's Iron County has a rich agricultural history, and it's celebrated every fall during the harvest season. The highlight of the festival is the Sheep Parade, where more than 1,000 sheep are herded down Cedar City's Main Street, along with antique tractors and vintage cars. This event celebrates the annual tradition of moving sheep and cattle from their high mountain summer ranges to the valley before winter arrives. Other fun events include a tractor pull, Dutch Oven cooking contest, cowboy poetry, a quilt show, and a ranch rodeo. This is a great event with good, wholesome, family-friendly fun.

3 Melon Days Festival

Third Weekend in September
O.K. Anderson City Park, 100 Solomon, Green River, UT 84525; 435-820-0592
melon-days.com

You might be surprised that anything grows in the deserts of East Utah, but Green River is the heart of Utah's melon farming region. Visit during the third week in September for this quaint celebration of all things pertaining to melons. Weekend events include a parade, live music, melon carving contests, golf tournament, softball tournament, pancake breakfasts, and the Melon Run. The parade features the world's largest watermelon slice, which is a parade float that once housed a watermelon stand. Of course, many vendors are on hand to sell food and souvenirs.

4 Ogden Twilight Concert Series

August & September
Ogden Amphitheater, 343 E 25th Street, Ogden, UT 84401
ogdentwilight.com

The Ogden Twilight Concert Series is a great way to close out the summer and enjoy the final warm days before winter. For a small-town festival, the acts that appear are quite well-known. The Flaming Lips, Deathcab for Cutie, and Portugal. The Man all played recently. Whether you opt for a season pass or individual shows, make sure you buy early; amazing prices ensure these tickets go fast!

5 Oktoberfest

Every Saturday, Sunday (and Labor Day) from Late August through Mid-October
9385 S Snowbird Center Drive, Snowbird, UT 84092; 1-800-232-9542
snowbird.com/oktoberfest/

This Bavarian-inspired festival is right at home on the slopes of Snowbird ski resort. Beginning the last weekend in August, revelers come from all over the West to enjoy traditional German music, family-friendly activities, food, and of course, lots of beer. Visit Der Marktplatz, with more than 30 vendors offering crafts for sale. In addition to the fun Oktoberfest events, guests can also partake in the summer activities of Snowbird, which include a mountain coaster, bungee trampolines, and an alpine slide. Admission to Oktoberfest is free (though there's a fee for parking), and the hours are from noon to 6:00 pm.

6 Park City Kimball Art Festival

Early August
Main Street, Park City, UT 84060; 435-649-8882
parkcitykimballartsfestival.org

Locals and visitors alike flock to this annual art festival held on Park City's Main Street. As one of the top-ranked art festivals in the country, more than 200 artists from around the country (as well as a few international artists) are invited to participate. Featured art comes in many forms, from photography, printmaking, sculpture, wood, glass, fiber, ceramics, and painting. A fun lineup of live music and food trucks rounds out this fun festival each summer. Advance ticket purchases are strongly recommended as this is a very popular event.

10

7, 9

8 Statewide

7 Park City Miners' Day

Early September
Main Street, Park City, UT 84060
parkcityminersday.org

While the rest of the country celebrates Labor Day, Park City gets more specific and celebrates Miners' Day. Mining is a huge part of Park City's history, and although most of the mines have closed, we still celebrate the miners that put Park City on the map. Starting with a parade, the festive day also includes mucking and drilling demonstrations and the Running of the Balls. This fundraising activity is a hit every year; attendees purchase numbered balls and watch them "run" down Main Street. This is a great way to close out the summer and celebrate Park City's mining heritage.

Park City Miners' Day celebrates the town's long ties to mining, such as this historic silver mine.

8 Pioneer Day

July 24th
Statewide

Mormon pioneers arrived in the Salt Lake Valley on July 24, 1847. More than 170 years later, most Utah towns pull out all the stops to celebrate Pioneer Day (or Pie-and-Beer day, as some non-Latter-day Saints residents have coined it). Fourth of July celebrations are just a warmup for the Pioneer Day celebrations, where each town has its own celebrations, often including parades and fireworks. It's a statewide holiday, and the Mormon Tabernacle Choir usually has a special performance to celebrate the occasion. If you're in Utah on July 24, make sure you find a local celebration and join in the fun.

9 Sundance Film Festival

Late January
Multiple venues in Park City and Salt Lake City, UT
sundance.org/festivals/sundance-film-festival/about

This is the premier film festival where independent films debut. Set mostly along Park City's Main Street, the town welcomes actors, producers, directors, and film enthusiasts from all over the globe. Since the festival's inception in 1985, many independent films debuted at Sundance have gone on to mainstream success. Whether you are a film buff or just want to people-watch, it's a great time to visit Park City, but the town's accommodations and restaurants book out pretty far in advance, so plan ahead!

10 Utah Arts Festival

Summer
Library Square, 200 E 400 S, Salt Lake City, UT 84101; 801-322-2428
uaf.org

Utah's largest outdoor festival features more than 150 visual artists and more than 100 performing artists. The festival started in 1977, celebraing more than 40 years of art celebration in Salt Lake City. Features include a marketplace, live music, performing arts, street theater, film, and literary arts. Three days of performances and exhibitions bring artists and patrons from all over the world to celebrate the arts scene in Utah.

11 Utah Festival Opera & Musical Theatre

June, July, August
Multiple venues in Logan, UT; 800-262-0074
utahfestival.org

Performers from around the world come to Logan in the summer to participate in world-class productions, giving Logan the nickname "Utah's Heart of the Arts." With more than 250 performances set in three historic theaters, there is always something to see if you visit Logan between late June and early August. Venues include the majestic Utah Theatre and the Ellen Eccles Theatre. This is an affordable way to experience big performances with a fantastic set and costume design, without breaking the bank. Logan is a quaint town in Northern Utah's Cache Valley, and Bear Lake is less than one hour away, through scenic Logan Canyon.

12 Utah Shakespeare Festival

June through October
Cedar City, UT; 800-PLAYTIX (752-9849)
www.bard.org

Celebrating 60 years in 2021, this legendary festival brings Shakespeare fans from all over the country to the Southern Utah University campus in Cedar City. This Tony Award-winning repertory theater stages multiple Shakespeare productions across three stages each summer and fall. The Engelstad Shakespeare Theatre is a modern version of the original Globe Theater where Shakespeare staged his early productions. In addition to rotating performances, additional special experiences include Play Orientations and Play Seminars where you can join theater scholars to discuss the previous day's performances. Don't miss the Shakespeare character garden outside; it's part of the larger SUU Art & Sculpture Stroll.

13 Utah State Fair

September
Utah State Fairpark, 155 N 1000 W, Salt Lake City, UT 84116; 801-538-8400
utahstatefair.com

Since 1856, Utah has thrown a State Fair to celebrate and showcase the state's agricultural achievements. Dozens of exhibits feature fine art, photography, floriculture, 4-H, and more. Entertainment is also plentiful, with lumberjack shows, comedians, and musical guests. Carnival rides and a rodeo are also a tradition at the fair. Of course, it's not a state fair if it doesn't have food! The Utah State Fair has the Beef Feast and plenty of other food vendors. A state fair is always a great way to experience the local culture, and that's certainly true in Utah!

14 Wasatch Wildflower Festival

July
Big Cottonwood Canyon and Little Cottonwood Canyon, UT; 801-930-5010
cottonwoodcanyons.org/event/wasatch-wildflower-festival

Spanning two weekends, this mobile festival hits each of the Salt Lake City area ski resorts in Big Cottonwood Canyon and Little Cottonwood Canyon. Timed to take advantage of peak alpine wildflower season, this festival is a great excuse for a trip to the mountains. Each location (Brighton, Solitude, Alta, and Snowbird) hosts a day of events that includes wildflower walks, kids' activities, music, and food. Volunteers are on hand to lead the walks and help educate visitors. The event is free, although you might also want to purchase a tram ticket at Snowbird, just for the amazing views!

Arnica Sunflowers in wildflowers season in the Wasatch Mountains

Rose Garden at Red Butte Garden

WHEN IT COMES TO NATURE, Utah is amazingly diverse. From the red rock deserts of the south to mountains more than 13,000 feet in the Uinta Mountains, there are all kinds of flora and fauna in Utah. With diverse landscapes come diverse climates, so there's always something in season in Utah.

GARDENS, FLOWERS, & ARBORETUMS

1 Ashton Gardens at Thanksgiving Point

3900 Garden Drive, Lehi, UT 84043; 801-768-4999
thanksgivingpoint.org/experience/ashton-gardens

Ashton Gardens features 50 acres of beautiful gardens, against a backdrop of Mount Timpanogos. Start at the Grand Allee and wind your way through more than a dozen themed gardens, including Monet Lake, a Fragrance Garden, an Italian Garden, and a Rose Garden. The annual spring Tulip Festival is extremely popular and features more than 300,000 tulip bulbs of many different varieties, including the Tulipa Thanksgiving Point, a special hybrid developed exclusively for the festival. The site also features the largest man-made waterfall in the Western Hemisphere. Visit the Trellis Cafe for lunch, and there's also a concession near the waterfall amphitheater. Golf cart rentals are available for those who prefer not to walk the entirety of the gardens. If you have time, another great Thanksgiving Point attraction is the Butterfly Biosphere, home to over 1,000 butterflies.

Ashton Gardens at Thanksgiving Point

2 Bear River Migratory Bird Refuge

2155 West Forest Street, Brigham City, UT 84302; 435-723-5887
fws.gov/refuge/bear_river_migratory_bird_refuge

More than 300 species of shore and water birds stop by this refuge throughout the year. Start your visit at the James V. Hansen Wildlife Education Center, where you can learn about the various birds you might see here. Next, follow the 1.5-mile trail through the wetlands near the visitor center. The highlight of this destination is the 12-mile Auto Tour Route, which also has an audio tour you can download ahead of your visit. Check the website for events and presentations as there are several special programs throughout the year. Surprisingly the refuge is just minutes off I-15, so it's a great place to take a break from driving and stretch your legs on the hiking trails.

3 Ogden Botanical Gardens

1750 Monroe Boulevard, Ogden, UT 84401; 801-399-8080
ogdenbotanicalgardens.org

This free public garden has a lovely location along the Ogden River in the foothills east of town. As part of Utah State University, the garden covers 11 acres, with nearly a dozen themed gardens. They include a rose garden, oriental garden, edible garden, pollinator garden, and cottage garden. There's also a small arboretum nearby, accessible a ways up the Ogden River pathway. There are benches and picnic tables scattered throughout the gardens, making this a lovely place for a picnic lunch among the flowers.

4 Red Butte Garden

300 Wakara Way, Salt Lake City, UT 84108; 801-585-0556
redbuttegarden.org

Set in the beautiful foothills near Emigration Canyon and the University of Utah, Red Butte Garden is one of the largest botanical gardens in the Intermountain West. Themed gardens like the Herb Garden, Fragrance Garden, and Rose Garden are popular spots to stop and smell the flowers. Several hiking trails lead out of the back of the property into the foothills, all with spectacular views of the Salt Lake Valley. The Summer Outdoor Concert Series is extremely popular, with artists like ZZ Top and the Counting Crows performing in the Red Butte amphitheater. The small gift shop also has some unique items to take home as a souvenir.

5, 6

5 State Arboretum of Utah

University of Utah campus, Salt Lake City, UT 84112; 801-581-7221
facilities.utah.edu/tree-tour

Dr. Walter P. Cottam was the co-founder of the Nature Conservancy as well as the chairman of the Botany Department at the University of Utah. His robust research and extensive collection led the state to name the campus as the official State Arboretum of Utah in 1961. The official University of Utah tree tour is a self-guided walk among the various species you can find on campus, including some record-holding trees of size and age. Whether you are looking for suitable trees to plant in your own home or are just looking for an interesting walk on the campus, this is a beautiful stroll. Using the interactive map, you can learn more about each type of tree.

6 Tracy Aviary and Botanical Garden

Liberty Park, 589 E 1300 S, Salt Lake City, UT 84105; 801-596-8500
tracyaviary.org

This cool spot is tucked into a corner of Salt Lake City's Liberty Park. In addition to seeing hundreds of different birds, from ducks to owls, Tracy Aviary also has several interactive shows and exhibits to entertain visitors. There are only two free-standing aviaries in the United States; Tracy Aviary is the oldest and largest, making this a unique experience you can only have in Salt Lake City. Dozens of enclosures house exotic and native birds, from the Australian kookaburra to Golden Eagles. At the Lorikeet Adventure, you can pay a small amount to hand-feed the lorikeets, which will land right on your arm. Daily presentations include an outdoor bird show, keeper talks, and interpretation stations. While you're here, check out the Bird Feeder Cafe, with drinks, snacks, and refreshing Dole Whip!

Lorakeet Adventure at Tracy Aviary and Botanical Garden

Dinosaur National Monument

UTAH IS A GEOLOGIST and paleontologist's dream. The sedimentary layers hold secrets millions of years old, and dinosaurs are a big theme in Utah. Every town seems to have a dinosaur museum with impressive collections. There is also a strong history of mining, which is still viable in many places around the state.

ROCKS & FOSSILS: DINOSAURS, MINES, & MORE

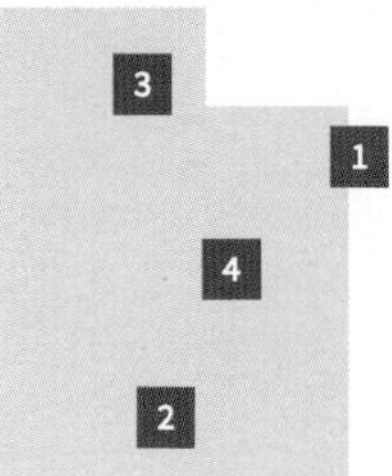

1 Dinosaur National Monument

11625 E 1500 S, Jensen, UT 84035; 435-781-7700
nps.gov/dino

This National Monument on the Utah-Colorado border has a lot going on! Start your visit on the Utah side at the Quarry Visitor Center where you'll hop a park shuttle to the Quarry Exhibit Hall. There are more than 1,500 fossils on display, showing nearly 150 million years of history. Next, follow the park road to view several petroglyph panels along the roadside and be amazed at the views from Split Mountain Campground. On the Colorado side, a singular scenic road leads to Harper's Corner, with a fantastic view of the Green River. Those with high-clearance vehicles can take Echo Park Road down to the river for a great view of Steamboat Rock. The monument has an extensive backcountry for those inclined to leave the beaten path. If you have more than a day, I highly recommend a whitewater float trip on the Green River.

2 Escalante Petrified Forest State Park

710 North Reservoir Road, Escalante, UT 84726; 435-826-4466
stateparks.utah.gov/parks/escalante-petrified-forest

This small state park is a great stop on the road between Bryce Canyon and Capitol Reef National Parks. The main attraction at this park is the petrified forest, featuring huge trees that were flooded, preserved, and petrified more than 130 million years ago. While there is a huge petrified log on display near the parking lot, the full effect is only gotten when hiking the park's interpretive trail. The Petrified Forest Trail is a 1-mile loop to the top of the mesa, and the Trail of Sleeping Rainbows adds another three-quarters of a mile to see the highest concentration of petrified wood in the area. The park also has a reservoir and a campground.

3 George S. Eccles Dinosaur Park

1544 E Park Boulevard, Ogden, UT 84401; 801-393-3466
dinosaurpark.org

This park includes three attractions for the price of one. Outside, the Dinosaur Park covers 5 acres and includes more than 100 life-size dinosaur sculptures. You'll also experience sound effects as you explore. Don't miss the volcano, cave, and dig quarry. There are also a couple of play areas with slides for the younger kids. Inside, they have the Elizabeth Dee Shaw Stewart Museum of Paleontology, with several fossils and skeletons, as well as a gem cave, where you can hunt for gems for an additional fee. Upstairs, visit the Ogden Natural History Museum's display of gemstones and minerals.

4 Jurassic National Monument

Dinosaur Quarry Road, Elmo, UT 84521; 435-636-3600
blm.gov/national-conservation-lands/utah/jurassic-national-monument

The Cleveland-Lloyd Dinosaur Quarry is a working dinosaur quarry and was recently designated as Jurassic National Monument. This central Utah location has the densest concentration of Jurassic-period dinosaur bones in the world. More than 70 individual dinosaurs have been identified at this site, from more than 12,000 bones. The most frequently found dinosaur at this site is the Allosaurus, one of the most common predators of the Jurassic period. More than 45 individual Allosaurus remains have been uncovered here. There's a small museum that is staffed, and an interpretive nature trail through some of the finds. While digging is not open to the public, you can peer in at the active dig site, which is protected by a small metal shed. Bring water and sunscreen as there is no shade along the trail. This site is part of a larger area called the Dinosaur Diamond, which includes the CEU Prehistoric Museum in Price, as well as the Museum of the San Rafael in Castle Dale. Plan for about 90 minutes each way from Price; the roads are not paved but in good condition.

Jurassic National Monument

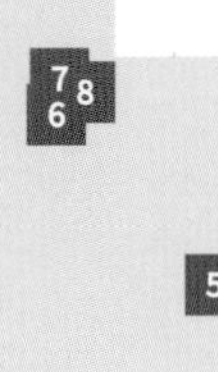

5 Moab Giants

112 UT 313, Moab, UT 84532; 435-355-0288
moabgiants.com

This open-air museum outside of Moab is perfect for anyone of any age who is obsessed with dinosaurs. Start your visit in the 3D movie theater, with a 10-minute film about the history of our planet. Next, head to the 5D prehistoric aquarium, a virtual underwater experience, unlike anything I've ever seen. In the Interactive Tracks Museum, you can learn about all different kinds of dinosaur tracks and how they are discovered. Take a quick trip up the view tower for an aerial view before setting off on the Dinosaur Trail. The half-mile trail winds through the desert and features dozens of life-size dinosaur replicas. There are also some fun sandbox digs along the way, as well as a playground, cafe, and gift shop.

Moab Giants

6 Museum of Ancient Life at Thanksgiving Point

2929 N Thanksgiving Way, Lehi, UT 84043; 801-768-2300
thanksgivingpoint.org/experience/museum-of-ancient-life

This Thanksgiving Point museum is chock full of dinosaur educational exhibits. With 60 complete dinosaur skeletons, this is the largest display of mounted dinosaurs in the world. Start your tour by learning about quarry sites, specifically the Bone Cabin Quarry near Medicine Bow, Wyoming. You can see how paleontologists work thanks to an open lab, and learn how coal and fossils are formed and how species become extinct. There are many kid-friendly exhibits, including a hands-on water table to explain erosion, as well as sandpits where kids can dig for fossils. There's also a movie theater, a junior paleo lab, a cafe, and a gift shop. Check the calendar for fun events like Tales for Tots storytime or Dirt on Dinos.

7 Natural History Museum of Utah

301 Wakara Way, Salt Lake City, UT 84108; 801-581-6927
nhmu.utah.edu

Perched along the Bonneville Shoreline Trail near Emigration Canyon on the University of Utah campus, the building is worth stopping to admire. The museum moved into its current location in 2012, in a modern copper-covered building meant to reflect the natural surroundings. Inside, you'll find engaging interactive exhibits and displays spread across four floors. In addition to natural history, they have exhibits on natural science, paleontology, anthropology, and more. The geology of Utah is particularly conducive to fossil preservation, so it's only fitting that Utah's Natural History Museum has more than 1.5 million specimens, including the largest display of ceratopsian skulls in the world. The dinosaur exhibit is particularly impressive and contains the only full Deinosuchus skeleton in the world; a unique catwalk design brings you face to face with this giant crocodile-like animal. Don't forget to stop and admire the interior architecture as well; designed to mimic Utah's canyons, it's a remarkable space with fantastic views of the surrounding mountains.

8 Park City Museum

528 Main Street, Park City, UT 84060; 435-649-7457
parkcityhistory.org

Located on Main Street in the heart of Park City's Old Town, the Park City Museum is a great first stop when you arrive in town. The museum is housed in the original City Hall and the Police and Fire Departments; in fact, you can step inside one of the old jail cells

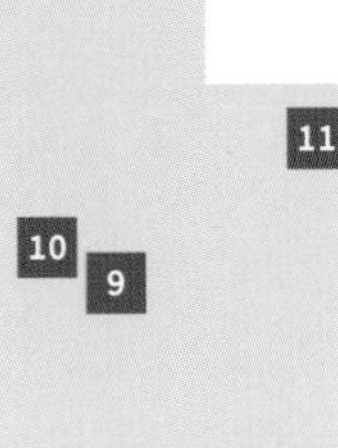

that's still in the basement. Several short films and interactive exhibits help paint a picture of the mines that put Park City on the map in the mid-nineteenth century, as well as the evolution into a world-class winter sports destination. Skiers of Park City Mountain and Deer Valley will see a lot of familiar names, as many ski runs are named after mines and claims. The museum has a map of all the claims in the area, as well as a 1926 fire truck.

9 Topaz Mountain

95 E 500 N, Fillmore, UT 84631; 435-743-3100
blm.gov/visit/topaz-mountain

An hour northwest of Delta in the West Desert of Utah, Topaz Mountain is one of the world's best places to find topaz. Located primarily within Bureau of Land Management boundaries, this is public land that anyone can access, provided they are adequately prepared to spend time in the barren desert with no services nearby. There is also an adventure company in the area that will take you out on a "recreational mining and prospecting tour." However you decide to visit, be ready to find all kinds of pink and salmon-colored topaz stones, as well as other gems and minerals.

10 U-Dig Fossils

Death Canyon Road, Delta, UT 84624; 435-864-3638
u-digfossils.com

Some "dig your own" fossil spots can feel cheesy or fake, but this spot in the West Desert is legit. Visitors have access to 40 acres of trilobite shale, and the owners excavate it often to turn up new fossils. Trilobites are an extinct marine species that shed their exoskeletons often, so there are endless fossils to discover. Your access fee includes tools, buckets, and on-site assistance if you need it. There are restrooms on-site, but not much else, so be sure to bring lots of water and snacks for as long as you plan to stay out. Best of all, you get to keep whatever you find.

Utah Field House of Natural History State Park Museum

11 Utah Field House of Natural History State Park Museum

496 Main Street, Vernal, UT 84078; 435-789-3799
stateparks.utah.gov/parks/utah-field-house

This collection is pretty impressive and indicative of why Vernal is also known as Utah's "Dinosaurland." The area around Vernal has been extremely productive for paleontologists and archeologists. A trip to this State Park Museum is a great precursor to venturing into the nearby Dinosaur National Monument. As soon as you enter the museum, you are greeted by a 90-foot-long dinosaur skeleton in the rotunda. Exhibits include a theater, fossil lab, Jurassic Hall, and a fluorescent minerals room, among others. Outside, dozens of dinosaur replicas line a garden walk through the museum grounds. The museum is also home to the local visitor center, so it's definitely a great first-stop in Dinosaurland.

Grafton Schoolhouse/Church

MINING WAS AND IS an important part of Utah's history and economy. The Gold Rush days brought many hopeful pioneers to the West, and many mines were opened throughout the state of Utah. While mining still plays an important part of Utah's economy and you can still see active mines throughout the state, the decline of some mines and other settlements has left several ghost towns scattered throughout. While there are more than 100 ghost towns in Utah, this is a small sampling of the most easily accessible ones that you can visit. If you have access to a four-wheel-drive vehicle, you can visit even more ghost towns in Utah.

GHOST TOWNS

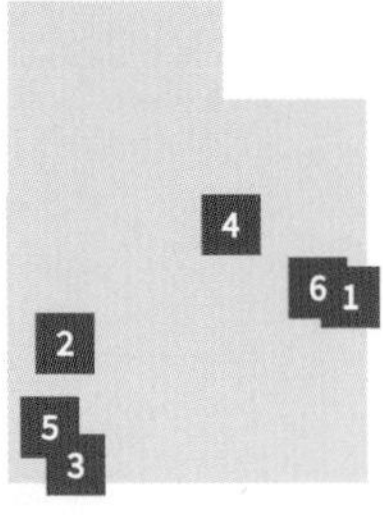

1 Cisco

Near I-70 and UT 128, Cisco, UT

If you're driving to Moab, take the scenic route along UT 128, which follows the Colorado River. Shortly after exiting the Interstate, take a short side trip to the ghost town of Cisco. Unlike many ghost towns, Cisco's history does not lie in mining, but rather it was once a stop for the railroads passing through here. As Moab tourism grew, Cisco was an important stopping point for weary travelers. Once the interstate system came along, the main route to Moab bypassed Cisco, rendering it a ghost town. Today, much of the town has been purchased by an artist who is attempting to create an artists' haven in the desert. You'll see some cool art installations around town. Cisco could be the next Marfa, so check it out before it's no longer a ghost town!

2 Frisco

UT 21/Ely Highway West of Milford, UT

Silver was discovered here in 1875, and the town quickly boomed around the resulting mine. It peaked with an estimated 6,000 residents and more than 20 saloons. Today, several buildings are scattered around the site, which can be tricky to find. Starting around 15 minutes from Milford, you'll see a historical marker on the north side of the highway. The cemetery is easiest to find and quite large, with many grave markers from the late nineteenth century through 1918. From here, you can see some old mining buildings up on the hill. Backtracking on the highway, take another dirt road near the "summit" marker to some old building foundations and the beehive kilns.

3 Grafton

Rockville, UT
graftonheritage.org

Located just 10 minutes from the small town of Rockville, this is allegedly one of the most photographed ghost towns in the West. Thanks to volunteers and donations, it's also very well preserved. The town was originally settled by Mormons in the mid-1800s, with a plan to grow cotton, a short-lived dream in this arid desert. Today, three homes and the church/schoolhouse remain in the town, and the cemetery containing Mormon and Paiute graves is located just down the road. The "newest" graves I saw were from 1911, but they are clearly still visited often, as evidenced by the coins and decorations left behind. This is definitely worth a quick detour on your way to Zion National Park.

4 Latuda

Helper, UT

This ghost town near Helper is one of Utah's "newest" ghost towns, as it was only founded around 1915 when a coal developer started the Liberty Fuel Company here. The town grew to an estimated 400 residents at the height of growth. Avalanches destroyed many homes, but they were rebuilt and once again thriving until the coal industry took a sharp decline in the mid-1950s and most residents moved elsewhere. Today, you can still see many buildings around the area, as well as foundations and a railroad trestle. The area is rumored to be haunted as well! From Helper, it's just 6.5 miles down a dirt road to this ghost town.

5 Old Iron Town

4128 S 17800 W, Cedar City, UT 84720

Located 22 miles west of Cedar City, this Utah ghost town holds the remains of what was once Iron City, or Iron Town. The town was founded in 1868 in an attempt to supply iron to the nearby Mormon settlements. The kiln and surrounding buildings, which included a schoolhouse and foundry, were abandoned after only 10 years as iron production moved elsewhere. Today, you can visit the site where the charcoal kiln remains. A short, interpretive trail winds through the ruins, giving you a picture of the town that once was.

6 Sego

Sego Canyon Road, Thompson Springs, UT 84540

Not far from I-70 near Green River, Sego Canyon is best known for panels of rock art dating back to 7000 B.C. However, the canyon is also home to the ghost town of Sego. Head north for half a mile past the rock art, and then turn east (right) on Sego Canyon Road. You'll first see the cemetery before continuing into the canyon where you'll start to see ruins of buildings. Sego was an important coal-mining town from about 1910 to 1955, and the population steadily declined through the 1950s. There are several building ruins and an old car scattered throughout the area. The dirt road is passable with a regular car when dry but does cross several washes.

Crystal Hot Springs

IN A STATE WITH SO MANY outdoor adventure opportunities, we are also blessed with several natural hot springs. Soaking in mineral water has been a popular holistic treatment for centuries; relatively recently, President Franklin D. Roosevelt sought out hot springs in Georgia to treat the effects of polio. Whether you hike to the hot springs or find a public spring to soak in after a day on the slopes, these mineral-rich hot springs are one of the best features of Utah!

HOT SPRINGS & MINERAL SPRINGS

2

5 4

3

1

1 Blue Lake Spring

15 miles south of Wendover, UT
travelnevada.com/water-sports/blue-lake

Unless you are off-roading, you'll have to travel through Nevada to get to this hidden spot in the western Utah desert. This geothermal pool is located 17 miles south of Wendover, with the last 8 miles on a bumpy dirt road that's suitable for passenger cars when dry. Surprisingly, this is a somewhat popular SCUBA diving spot, and my GPS directed me right to the "Blue Lake SCUBA dock." The last 100 yards or so to the lake are on an older wooden boardwalk, so you'll park and walk the plank until you reach the lake. A fishing dock and ladder stairs have been installed in the lake for easier access. During the summer months, mosquitoes, horseflies and potential algae blooms are something for which you should prepare.

2 Crystal Hot Springs

8215 UT 38, Honeyville, UT 84314; 435-339-0038
crystalhotsprings.net/home

Located just off I-15 near Logan and Brigham City in Northern Utah, Crystal Hot Springs has been open for business since 1901. With the highest mineral content spring in the world, people flock from all over the world to soak in Crystal Hot Springs. Today, you'll find an Olympic-size swimming pool, a large soaker pool, three mineral hot tubs, and two huge waterslides. Your entry fee allows access to all of the pools, although the waterslides are an additional $2. They have a small gift shop on-site, and you can rent a locker and pool towel for the day. On-site camping is also available from March 1 through October 31.

3 Fifth Water Hot Springs

Diamond Fork Road, Spanish Fork, UT
utah.com/hiking/fifth-waterfalls-trail

If you want picturesque hot springs in the secluded woods, this is the perfect hot spring. Reaching these soaking pools requires a 2.5-mile hike, but that doesn't deter crowds from arriving on the weekends.

There are three waterfalls along the trail, as well as several pools where you can adjust the temperature with water from the adjacent creek. This can turn into a bit of a party scene in the evening, and be prepared to encounter nude soakers. If you plan to visit with kids, go earlier in the morning for a more family-friendly environment. The pools get hotter as you climb, so work your way up as you adjust to the temperatures. In winter, seasonal road closures add up to 8 miles round-trip, and microspikes may be needed to safely hike this trail.

4 Homestead Crater

700 N Homestead Drive, Midway, UT 84049; 435-657-3840
homesteadresort.com/things-to-do/homestead-crater

As part of the Midway Geothermal Area, these springs are the perfect place for an apres-ski soak. A group of Swiss immigrants settled here in the late nineteenth century and discovered a mysterious rock structure secreting warm water on their land. Thus, the hot spring was discovered inside a calcite dome that is nearly 60 feet high. A resort was built up around the spring, but the crater remains pretty close to its original form as it was discovered. To visit the crater, you just need to reserve a time slot to soak. You'll have 40 minutes to enjoy the warm mineral waters while gazing up at the sky through a hole in the top of the crater. You can also SCUBA dive or snorkel in the crater. If you visit in winter, the Midway Ice Castles are also located on the grounds of the Homestead Resort. Book early as both attractions fill up quickly!

5 Inlet Park Hot Springs

6800 N Saratoga Road, Saratoga Springs, UT 84045; 801-866-9793
saratogaspringscity.com

Sometimes called Saratoga Springs, these hot spring pools sit on the edge of Utah Lake, sandwiched between a city park and a housing development. From the parking lot at Inlet Park, follow the paved trail southwest of the parking lot for about 8 minutes to reach the two pools, which are quite hot. Be prepared for muddy conditions, and it can be quite buggy in the summertime. Although this feels like it's remote, it's apparently patrolled quite often by the local police, so pay attention to the park hours and make sure you're out before the park closes. Inlet Park is also the southern end of the Jordan River Parkway, so it's a great destination for cyclists to enjoy a soak during a ride.

6 Meadow Hot Springs

Meadow, UT
utah.com/things-to-do/outdoor-recreation/hot-springs/meadow-hot-springs

These are some of the most unique hot springs in Utah, as they are totally camouflaged by the surrounding fields. You'll have to follow your GPS because the gravel road leading to the springs is not labeled. The pools are just 10 minutes from the Meadow exit off I-15, and there's a small parking lot and donation box letting you know you've arrived. After a short hike down a bumpy dirt road, you'll come upon the first of three hot pools, each averaging around 100°F. There are no facilities here, so come in your bathing suit or be prepared to change in your car. Although these hot springs sit on private property, they are open to the public as long as visitors continue to respect the property owners.

7 Mystic Hot Springs

475 E 100 North, Monroe, UT 84754; 435-527-3286
mystichotsprings.com

These hot springs come out of the mountain at 168°F and then cascade into several pools on the property, including a handful of cast-iron bathtubs that appear to be melted into the mountainside, thanks to mineral buildup that is absorbing the tubs. You must purchase a 2-hour soaking pass ahead of time online, and they do sell out, especially on the weekends, so plan ahead. It's definitely a unique location with an old-school hippie vibe, and they have a stage set up for live music and events in the summer. They have converted some old buses into overnight accommodation, but the campground is a little rough around the edges, so I would skip that and stay in nearby Richfield.

Mystic Hot Springs

8 Veyo Pool Resort

287 E Veyo Resort Road, Veyo, UT 84782; 435-574-2300
veyopool.com

Just 25 minutes north of St. George, this private resort features an all-natural spring-fed swimming pool. With depths ranging from 3 feet to 7 feet, this is a popular spot for local families to enjoy a day in the pool. The water is not hot, but a nice swimming temperature. The concession stand sells food, pool floats, and toys, and they host a biweekly movie night in the summer. There's also a rustic campground on-site, as well as a rental home. The canyon walls hold climbing routes, and the creek has lots of crawdads that you can easily catch. If you are not camping on-site, you'll park at the top of a small hill and walk down the road to the pool entrance.

Odgen Temple

MORMONS AND UTAH go hand in hand, as Mormons were some of the first white settlers to arrive in Utah and have been responsible for founding many of Utah's cities, including Salt Lake City. As Mormons fled west from religious persecution in Illinois, they arrived in the Salt Lake Valley in 1847 and quickly established communities throughout the state. Today, members of The Church of Jesus Christ of Latter-day Saints make up more than half of Utah's population. There are many places in Utah where you can learn about the arrival of the church and the settling of the Beehive State.

LDS HISTORY, LANDMARKS, & CULTURE

2, 3

1

1 Cove Fort

Highway 161 SE, Beaver, UT 84713; 435-438-5547
churchofjesuschrist.org/learn/historic-sites/utah/cove-fort

Cove Fort was founded in 1867 when the Hinckley family was directed to set up an outpost of The Church of Jesus Christ of Latter-day Saints at what was quickly becoming a crossroads as more settlers moved south from Salt Lake City. Intended to protect the mail, travelers, and telegraphs passing through, the fort remained an active hub of activity for 20 years before it was leased, then sold. Today, it has been restored by the church and is open to visitors. Start your tour with a short video introduction of the fort before setting off to explore the exhibits. The fort rooms have been restored to show how they would have received guests back in the day. Missionaries are on hand to provide commentary, or you can go through at your own pace.

2 Temple Square

50 N Temple, Salt Lake City, UT 84150; 801-240-8945
churchofjesuschrist.org/feature/templesquare

Temple Square is the World Headquarters of The Church of Jesus Christ of Latter-day Saints. This is also the final stop on the Mormon Pioneer National Historic Trail, which covers five states from Illinois to Nevada. Temple Square is the point of origin for all city quadrants as the street numbers all emanate from the Temple. The five-block square encompasses 35 acres of beautifully manicured lawns and gardens and several important buildings for the church and its members. Free tours are given daily in up to 40 languages. In the summer, garden tours and concerts in the park are also offered. A few of the key sights at Temple Square include:

- **Salt Lake Temple**—Non-church members are not allowed inside, but it's a beautiful building to admire from the outside.
- **Tabernacle**—Don't miss the chance to watch the world-famous Mormon Tabernacle Choir rehearse, which is typically on Thursday evenings and open to the public.
- **Family History Library**—Search the largest genealogical collection in the world for free! Some records are stored in a vault in the

mountains, so you can do some research ahead of time and request the records to be available for you.

- **Lion House Pantry**—Housed in a former residence of Brigham Young, this is a popular restaurant for members of the church and visitors.
- **North and South Visitor Centers** have interactive exhibits and films where you can learn more about the church and how they came to settle in Utah.

3 This is The Place Heritage Park

2601 E Sunnyside Avenue, Salt Lake City, UT 84108; 801-582-1847
thisistheplace.org

Learn about Mormon pioneers and how they settled the Salt Lake valley after fleeing Nauvoo, Illinois, on what's now known as the Mormon Trail. Upon reaching this spot at the mouth of Emigration Canyon, Brigham Young declared, "This is the right place; drive on." Today, many pioneer buildings have been relocated and reconstructed into a living history farm, where visitors can learn about the pioneer spirit of the nineteenth century. A train ferries visitors around the park to various buildings, including a drugstore, pottery shop, blacksmith shop, and various individual homes. Grab a bite to eat at the Huntsman Hotel, ice cream parlor, or Brigham Young's Donut Shop. Try your hand at milking a cow or schedule a horseback ride in the surrounding foothills. There's also a petting zoo, playground, and extensive gift shop. In a nod to the original occupants of this region, there's also an American Indian village on a hill overlooking the park.

This is the Place Heritage Park

American West Heritage Center

WHILE THE MAJORITY of Utah attractions are outdoors, there are some excellent museums to check out while you're here. With the largest household size in the nation, Utah is known for large families, which results in many family-friendly attractions. No matter what part of the state you find yourself, you're bound to find museums dedicated to Utah history, nature, science, and art, as well as some world-class children's museums. You just never know what kind of museum you're going to stumble on when traveling through Utah.

Ft. Douglas
Military Mus.
This Is The Place
Heritage Park
Utah's Hogle
Zoo
Westminster Coll.
186
134
80
Mountain
Dell Res.
Parleys
WASATCH
Cr.

MUSEUMS & ZOOS

Living Planet Aquarium

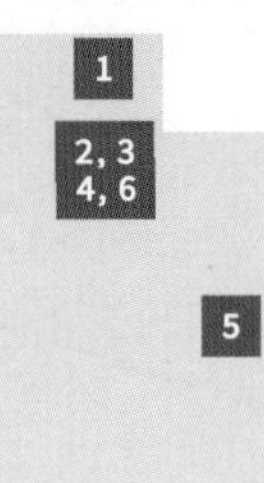

1 American West Heritage Center

4025 S US 89, Wellsville, UT 84339; 435-245-6050
awhc.org

With a focus on the years from 1820 to 1920, this living history museum and farm explores the diverse cultures that settled the Cache Valley. Starting inside the Cache Valley history museum, you can read about the American Indians who lived here and how conflict with settlers ultimately led to the Bear River Massacre in 1863. Outside, there are 275 acres of farmland and reconstructed villages. Make sure you grab a map at the entrance, as the site is quite large! There are animals everywhere, plus pony rides, miniature train rides, and concessions. Spring and fall are full of fun events at the farm. People from all over Utah come to visit in April for Baby Animal Days!

2 Clark Planetarium

110 S 400 W, Salt Lake City, UT 84101; 385-468-7827
slco.org/clark-planetarium

This highly interactive museum at first feels more like a video game arcade than a museum. Admission to the main exhibits is free, while there is a small fee for the programs in the two theaters. The Northrop Grumman IMAX Theater and the Hansen Dome Theater both have 40-minute programs throughout the day. Exhibits are divided into Earth, Near Earth, and Beyond. Look for special events throughout the year and don't miss the Planet Fun Store.

3 Discovery Gateway Children's Museum

444 W 100 S, Salt Lake City, UT 84101; 801-456-5437
discoverygateway.org

Children of all ages will find inspiration at this hands-on museum. Exhibits include a bank, grocery store, auto mechanic shop, water table, a STEAM lab, and studio, plus a BeeHive climbing area. There's also a reading nook, a sensory room, and a Life Flight helicopter and rescue hangar on the roof. With lots of room for kids to run, this is a great place to escape the summer heat and have fun indoors. Special programs include reading to a therapy dog, a sensory room, and sensory backpacks.

4 Farm Country at Thanksgiving Point

3003 N Thanksgiving Way, Lehi, UT 84043; 801-768-2300
thanksgivingpoint.org/experience/farm-country

It's a rare opportunity to visit a working farm in the middle of the city, but that's exactly what Farm Country offers. Visitors have the chance to feed and pet some of the animals and learn about farm chores through hands-on activities and exhibits. Your admission ticket includes a pony ride for children and a wagon ride for everyone. Some of the most popular exhibits include the rabbit hutch, duck pond, and the Junior Master Gardeners program. The farm is also available for special events like weddings and birthdays. In the spring, the farm loves to show off its baby animals and usually hosts a "baby animal birthday party" in mid-May.

5 John Wesley Powell River History Museum

1765 E Main Street, Green River, UT 84525; 435-564-3427
johnwesleypowell.com

If you've ever spent time on a river trip in the West or plan to in the future, a visit to this museum is a must. John Wesley Powell was a geologist and is most famous for his 1860 expedition down the Green and Colorado Rivers of the American West. The museum explores his various expeditions, as well as the sport of river rafting. You can see how the whitewater raft and wooden dories have evolved over the years. As home to the River Runners Hall of Fame, you can learn about various players in the field, including George Wendt, founder of OARS, one of the top whitewater rafting companies in the West. There's also an art gallery, dinosaur exhibit, short film, and a gift shop with an extensive selection of books.

6 Loveland Living Planet Aquarium

12033 Lone Peak Parkway, Draper, UT 84020; 801-355-3474
thelivingplanet.com

From the frigid waters of the Antarctic to the dry riverbeds of Utah, Utah's largest aquarium covers it all. While the majority of exhibits are indoors, there's also a great outdoor space at the aquarium as well, marked by a huge mysterious claw-like structure. It's actually an old stage prop from a U2 Concert tour that was purchased by the aquarium. There's a coral reef playground, migration zipline, and water tables among other outdoor attractions. Exhibits are grouped by geographic area, including South America, Discover Utah, and Antarctic Adventure. At the Penguin Research Station, watch dozens of Gentoo penguins toddling around and entertaining the crowds. The shark tunnel is another cool feature, with sharks and giant stingrays swimming overhead. Special experiences such as penguin and shark encounters are not scheduled every day, so reserve a spot ahead of time.

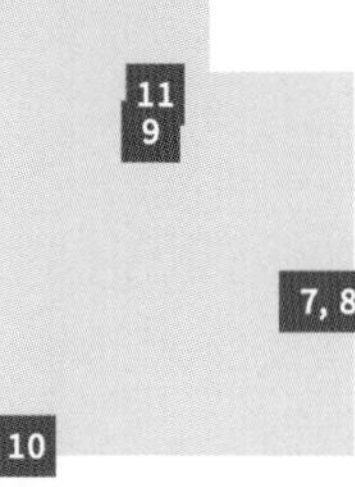

7 Moab Museum

118 E Center Street, Moab, UT 84532; 435-259-7985
moabmuseum.org

Admittedly, most Moab attractions are of the outdoor adventure variety. That has not always been the case, though, and this small museum is a nice break from the more athletic pursuits nearby. Just a block off Main Street, the Moab Museum offers a compelling walk back through time. The trip starts with the Indigenous people groups who have lived here for thousands of years, is followed by the short-lived Mormon settlement in 1855 and leads to the more-recent development of Moab as the "Uranium Capital of the World" in the 1950s. Learn how Moab used tourism to come back from the brink of extinction and how tourism plays a role in the local economy and ecosystems today. There's even a fun display of how rafting, mountain biking, and rock climbing equipment have evolved over the years.

8 Moab Museum of Film & Western Heritage

Red Cliffs Lodge; Mile 14, UT 128, Moab, UT 84532; 435-259-2002
redcliffslodge.com/the-lodge/moab-museum-of-film-and-western-heritage

This free museum is located in the basement of the Red Cliffs Lodge and offers a fun look at the history of movie making in the Moab area. The Moab to Monument Valley Film Commission is the longest ongoing film commission in the world. Most famously, *Thelma and Louise* was filmed here, and the museum includes a short film about the final scene, which was filmed at Dead Horse Point State Park. The museum has film memorabilia from some of the more than 120 movies, TV shows, and commercials that were filmed in the area, dating back to 1925.

9 Museum of Natural Curiosity

3605 Garden Drive, Lehi, UT 84043; 801-768-2300
thanksgivingpoint.org/experience/museum-of-natural-curiosity

Located next to the Ashton Gardens at Thanksgiving Point, this children's museum includes more than 400 interactive experiences for all ages. The Rainforest has ancient ruins and chambers that kids can crawl through before moving on to Water Works, where they can learn about water, wind, sun, and earth. For an additional fee, you can try out the ropes course suspended 40 feet above the museum floor. Kidopolis is a child-sized village where they can learn everyday tasks at the vet clinic, auto shop, bank, movie studio, and farm. Outside, the Discovery Garden has a playground, cave, waterfall, and a koi pond.

10 Rosenbruch World Wildlife Museum

1835 S. Convention Center Drive, St. George, UT 84790; 435-656-0033
rosenbruch.org

Local resident Jim Rosenbruch has grown what started out as a private collection of St. George into a natural history museum whose mission is conservation and appreciation of the world's wildlife. It is an homage to the art of taxidermy, with dozens of dioramas featuring more than 300 species of mammals, birds, and insects from around the world. Admission includes an electronic audio tour featuring stories from Rosenbruch himself. Each diorama features realistic surroundings, including audio accompaniment. Other attractions include a kids' room, insect room, and a gift shop. This is a great place to escape the summer heat in St. George for a few hours!

11 The Leonardo

209 E 500 S, Salt Lake City, UT 84111; 801-531-9800
theleonardo.org

A true homage to the curiosity and genius of Leonardo da Vinci, this Salt Lake City museum sparks the imagination with dozens of interactive exhibits. Visitors get the unique opportunity to see how science, technology, art, and creativity are all connected. Start at Flight, the flagship exhibit about air travel and its ties to Utah, which also includes a real C-131 and a Russian MIG-21 that were rescued from the airplane boneyard in Arizona. The Mines to Vines is an exhibit about Princess Diana's tireless work to bring awareness to and eradicate landmines around the world. The museum does a great job of balancing out exhibits aimed at younger visitors with those that can be appreciated by adults. There's also a bookstore and cafe, as well as special classes and events regularly scheduled throughout the year, including summer camps for kids.

12

12 Utah's Hogle Zoo

2600 Sunnyside Avenue S, Salt Lake City, UT 84108; 801-584-1700
hoglezoo.org

Set in the foothills of the Wasatch Mountains at the mouth of Emigration Canyon, Utah's Hogle Zoo is a great place to spend a sunny afternoon in Salt Lake City. The zoo started more than 100 years ago with a small collection of animals in Liberty Park. Local children raised money to purchase an elephant named Princess Alice from the circus, and after too many successful escapes, the zoo decided to find the elephant and its other animals a proper home. In 1931, the zoo moved to its current location on land donated by the Hogle family. Today, Utah's Hogle Zoo is accredited by the Association of Zoos & Aquariums and is an active participant in the AZA's Species Survival Plan. The zoo features more than 800 animals housed on the 42-acre property, in areas such as Rocky Shores, African Savanna, Elephant Encounter, Primate Forest, and Asian Highlands. In addition to the exhibits, the Zoo has a train, a carousel, and a play area. In 2020, a baby Western Lowland Gorilla named Georgia was born at the zoo. Visitors can take part in special animal encounters, which help raise money for animals in the wild. There's also a fun calendar of annual events that includes an art show, BooLights!, Zoo Brew, and more! Several on-site dining options allow you to make this a full-day excursion.

Grizzly bear at Hogle Zoo

Monarch Cave in Bears Ears National Moument

AMERICAN INDIAN CULTURE runs deep in Utah, with many different tribes calling present-day Utah home. The five major tribes in Utah are the Ute, Navajo, Paiute, Goshute, and Shoshone. These bands of Utah American Indians are as diverse as the landscapes of Utah; the Navajo Nation extends into southern Utah from Arizona, while the Shoshone live in the more mountainous region that Utah shares with Wyoming. If you want to learn about current or historic American Indian culture, there are many places to do so in Utah.

AMERICAN INDIAN CULTURE

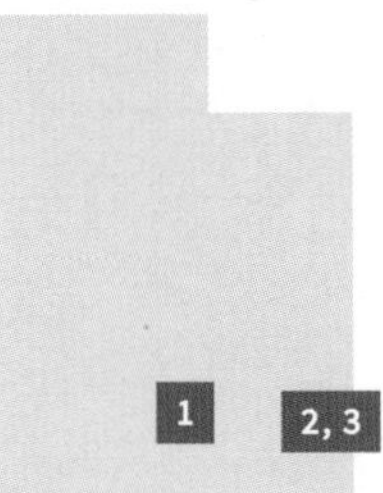

1 Anasazi State Park Museum

60 UT 12, Boulder, UT 84716; 435-335-7308
stateparks.utah.gov/parks/anasazi

This is a great stop to break up the drive between Bryce Canyon National Park and Capitol Reef National Park. The museum has preserved several ruins from an ancient Anasazi village as well as a reconstructed replica home that you can go inside. This is estimated to be one of the largest communities in the area at the time of occupation around 1,000 years ago. Inside the museum, there are several displays with artifacts from the original site, including pottery, clothing, and arrowheads. There's also a park store with souvenirs and often a food truck in the parking lot.

2 Bears Ears National Monument

365 N Main, Monticello, UT 84535; 435-587-1500
fs.usda.gov/visit/bears-ears-national-monument

Named for towering twin buttes rising from the desert floor, Bears Ears is a special place for all who visit, especially those who call the area home. Artifacts here date back to the Clovis period, and many pueblos and cliff dwellings were left behind by the Ancestral Puebloans (Anasazi) and the Fremont people, among others. Within Bears Ears, you'll find natural bridges and arches, petroglyphs, and ruins. Hiring an American Indian guide to show you around the area is highly recommended; not only will you learn so much more about the history and the people who lived here, but you'll also ensure that you are visiting respectfully. Louis Williams at Ancient Wayves grew up on the nearby Navajo reservation and offers customized tours from half-day to multi-day hikes and rafting trips. Some of the highlights to see in Bears Ears include the following:

- **Butler Wash below Comb Ridge** has several ruin sites and petroglyph panels
- **Butler Wash Dinosaur Track Site**
- **Sand Island Petroglyph panel near Bluff**
- **Mule Canyon House on Fire ruins**
- **Mule Canyon Kiva**

House on Fire

3 Edge of the Cedars State Park Museum

660 W 400 N, Blanding, UT 84511; 435-678-2238
stateparks.utah.gov/parks/edge-of-the-cedars

Any visit to the southeast corner of Utah (Utah's Canyon Country) should begin at this museum. Start with a short film introduction of the region before touring the museum's extensive collection of artifacts and photographs. Learn about the various archaeological sites in the region, some of which were just discovered by families out for a hike! The museum has one of the largest collections of Anasazi (Ancestral Puebloan) pottery in the southwestern United States, as well as the only known Macaw feather sash, which dates back to around 1100 AD. Behind the museum, you can tour a restored Puebloan village and even climb down into a kiva. This museum provides a great foundation for exploring the region's canyons and ruins.

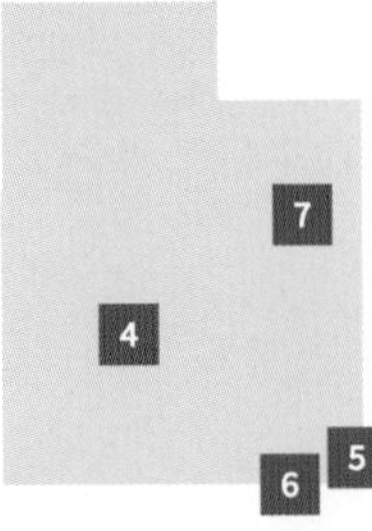

4 Fremont Indian State Park and Museum

3820 W Clear Creek Canyon Road, Sevier, UT 84766; 435-527-4631
stateparks.utah.gov/parks/fremont-indian

The Fremont Indians, or Moki, were some of the earliest-known settlers in the southwestern United States. They began to cultivate crops around 2,000 years ago in addition to hunting and gathering. Clear Creek Canyon, where this State Park Museum is located, was one of the largest Fremont communities ever discovered. Inside, there is a nicely curated museum of various artifacts from the Fremont people, traders on the Old Spanish Trail, and miners. Outside, there are several hiking trails and attractions, including several petroglyph panels. In addition to the museum, the park also has two campgrounds. This is a popular park for ATVs and, with 4WD, you can access Kimberly ghost town about 9 miles up the canyon.

5 Hovenweep National Monument

About 45 miles west of Cortez, CO. See website for directions;
970-562-4282 ext. 10
nps.gov/hove/index.htm

This is one of many spots in Utah where you can walk among prehistoric ruins. Set just on the border of Colorado, just 1 hour from Mesa Verde National Park, Hovenweep National Monument is what remains of six Ancestral Puebloan villages spread across a 20-mile area. The structures you see today are from the cultural period following Mesa Verde. If you visit both, perhaps you can see the evolution and adaptation. The Utah visitor center and campground are located in the Square Tower Group, which has the largest collection of structures in the monument. Take the Little Ruin Trail, a 2-mile loop trail taking you past the largest and most well-preserved ruins. A small campground is available year-round on a first-come, first-served basis.

6 Monument Valley Navajo Tribal Park

Indian Route 42, Oljato-Monument Valley, AZ 84536; 435-727-5870
navajonationparks.org/tribal-parks/monument-valley

One of the Southwest's most iconic landscapes, Monument Valley straddles the Utah-Arizona border near the Four Corners area. In the 1930s, Hollywood director John Ford visited Monument Valley and subsequently filmed several movies here. More recently, films like Easy Rider and Forrest Gump have imprinted the monuments into American film history. The Valley, managed by the Navajo Nation, remains largely untouched, with only a dirt road circling the sandstone monuments. Private vehicles are allowed on the 17-mile loop road, which is suitable for passenger vehicles in good weather. However, many tours are offered, including several that visit areas otherwise restricted to visitors. Nearby facilities include The View Hotel inside the park and Goulding's Trading Post and Lodge just outside the park.

7 Nine Mile Canyon

Carbon County, UT
carbonutah.com/attraction/nine-mile-canyon

Located in what is called the Carbon Corridor, Nine Mile Canyon is sometimes called the "world's longest art gallery." Featuring (more than nine!) miles of Fremont, Ute, and Archaic petroglyphs and granaries in addition to a fantastic scenic drive, this remote spot is definitely worth a detour as you drive through eastern Utah. There are pullouts, trailheads, and spotting scopes all along the 46-mile road. Some spots, like Daddy Canyon and the Big Hunt, require a short walk to reach the petroglyphs. Make sure to download a map ahead of time, as cell service is limited and not all spots are clearly marked from the road. If you approach from Duchesne or Myton in the north, expect about an hour on unpaved roads that should be suitable for passenger cars in dry weather. Approaching from the south, the road is paved all the way from the town of Wellington.

The Great Hunt Petroglyph Panel at Nine Mile Canyon

Dead Horse Point State Park

BESIDES UTAH'S FIVE NATIONAL PARKS, there are tons of cool places designated as national monuments or state parks in the state. From places of great natural beauty to educational museums and parks, Utah has so many amazing resources and things to do with a national parks or a state parks pass.

NATIONAL MONUMENTS & STATE PARKS

Long Canyon in Grand Staircase-Escalante National Monument

2
1
3
4

1 Antelope Island State Park

4528 W 1700 S, Syracuse, UT 84075; 801-725-9263
stateparks.utah.gov/parks/antelope-island

This is the best (and nearest) place to visit the Great Salt Lake from Salt Lake City. The island is accessed via the Davis County Causeway near the town of Layton. Best known for the buffalo herd that has lived here since 1893, the south tip of the island also offers spectacular views back to the Salt Lake City skyline and a historic homestead at the Fielding Garr Ranch. Other wildlife often spotted here include coyotes, pronghorn antelope, mule deer, badgers, and porcupines. At the north end of the island, you'll find the visitor center, two campgrounds, a beach, and concessions. The park has several miles of hiking, biking, and horseback trails, with guided e-bike tours and rentals available through Antelope E-Bikes.

Buffalo Herd at Antelope Island State Park

2 Bear Lake State Park

940 N Bear Lake Boulevard, Garden City, UT 84028; 435-946-3343
stateparks.utah.gov/parks/bear-lake

This Caribbean-blue lake is the secret vacation spot for locals in northeast Utah and southeast Idaho. Minerals in the water give it a turquoise color and the nickname of the "Caribbean of the Rockies." This is a year-round destination for locals. In the summer, boats, jet-skis, and beachgoers fill the area, while winter brings ice fishing and snowmobiling. The state park has three districts on the Utah side of the lake. Both Rendezvous Beach on the southern end of the lake and the marina on the east have beaches and watercraft rentals. The east side is quieter with rocky beaches. Several campgrounds and rental homes line the shores, and the nearby town of Garden City has plenty of tourist services, including world-famous raspberry shakes!

3 Cedar Breaks National Monument

UT 143, Brian Head, UT 84719; 435-986-7120
nps.gov/cebr/index.htm

If you are looking for a less-crowded alternative to Bryce Canyon National Park, this is it. At an elevation of more than 10,000 feet, it's also a cool respite from the surrounding desert. Experience beautiful red sandstone hoodoos in the canyon, which is more than 2,000 feet deep. Explore hiking trails along the rim, dark night skies, and deep snow in the winter, which is perfect for snowshoeing, cross-country skiing, or snowmobiling. A new visitor center facility was recently approved and will offer more educational opportunities for visitors. The monument also features one campground, while more services are available in Brian Head or Cedar City. The road may be closed at times in winter, so be sure to call ahead for current road conditions.

4 Coral Pink Sand Dunes State Park

12500 Sand Dune Road, Kanab, UT 84741; 435-648-2800
stateparks.utah.gov/parks/coral-pink

This state park near Kanab in southern Utah is a great lesson in geology and erosion, as you can see red sandstone cliffs and the resulting pink sand dunes below. This park is super popular with ATV and off-highway vehicle riders, as 90 percent of the park is open to them, and guided tours are also available through Coral Pink ATV Tours. A scenic overlook is available within a short walk of the day-use parking lot, while the park rents sandboards and sleds for use on the dunes. There's also a campground with electric hookups, restrooms, and hot showers.

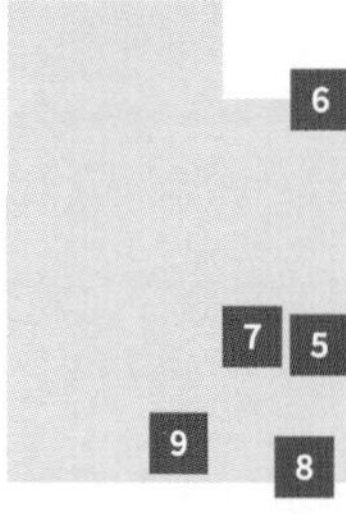

5 Dead Horse Point State Park

UT 313, Moab, UT 84532; 435-259-2614
stateparks.utah.gov/parks/dead-horse

Set between Arches National Park and Canyonlands National Park outside of Moab, this state park is every bit as stunning as the national parks, albeit on a much smaller scale. Start with the scenic drive through the park, ending at Dead Horse Point Overlook. Enjoy the astounding views in every direction before circling back to the Visitor Center, where several hiking trails begin. The park also has mountain biking trails, two campgrounds, and two yurt villages with overnight accommodations. The entrance to Dead Horse Point State Park is along the road to Canyonlands Island in the Sky district, so it's a quick and easy side trip that is well worth the detour.

6 Flaming Gorge National Recreation Area

25 UT 43, Manila, UT 84046; 435-789-1181
fs.usda.gov/detail/ashley/specialplaces/?cid=stelprdb5212203

This reservoir gets its name from the flaming red rocks towering above the shoreline. The reservoir was created in 1964 when the Flaming Gorge dam was constructed. There's a visitor center at the dam, which offers tours from April through October. Gateway towns with services, rentals, and tours are Manila and Dutch John. Boating, jet skiing, and house boating are all popular activities at the reservoir. It's also known for trophy lake trout, with the state record set here at 53 pounds! There are more than 40 campgrounds in the area and miles of hiking, biking, and OHV trails. The Flaming Gorge-Uintas National Scenic Byway has interpretive signs that tell you through which geological era you are driving, and there's a free audio tour you can download.

7 Goblin Valley State Park

Goblin Valley Road, Green River, UT 84525; 435-275-4584
stateparks.utah.gov/parks/goblin-valley

Despite its remote location between Capitol Reef National Park and Moab, this unique state park is very popular. Hoodoos are a common feature in many of Utah's parks, but these hoodoos are more "goblin-like," hence the name. The landscape here is often compared to Mars, and there is even a Mars training center not far away from where scientists can replicate the landscape. Goblin Valley State Park features 6 miles of hiking trails and 7 miles of biking trails within the Wild Horse Trail System. It is also a designated Dark Sky Park, which is best experienced with an overnight stay. The park has one campground with 25 camping sites, two yurts, and a flying disc golf course.

8 Goosenecks State Park

UT 316 Mexican Hat, UT 84531; 435-678-2238
stateparks.utah.gov/parks/goosenecks

This state park is truly a hidden gem in the southeast corner of Utah. While many travelers flock to Horseshoe Point in Arizona or Deadhorse Point State Park in Utah, the best river views are here at Goosenecks State Park. The park is small, so it's an easy detour between Monument Valley and Bluff or Blanding. Step up to the scenic overlook and gaze down more than 1,000 feet to multiple goosenecks in the San Juan River. It is truly a stunning example of erosion and geology.

9 Grand Staircase-Escalante National Monument

745 US 89, Kanab, UT 84741; 435-826-5499
blm.gov/programs/national-conservation-lands/utah/grand-staircase-escalante-national-monument

This National Monument is larger than the state of Delaware, covering a huge swath of land from the Arizona border to Glen Canyon and Capitol Reef National Park. Although much of the monument's treasures are hidden in the backcountry, there is still plenty to enjoy on a day trip through the area. US 89 and Scenic Byway 12 are two scenic roads through the area, while scenic viewpoints along the way really give you a sense of why this is called the Grand Staircase. Long Canyon has, ironically enough, a short slot canyon close to the road if you're short on time, while Spooky and Peek-a-Boo Canyons are accessible via short hikes, although a high clearance vehicle is recommended for the rocky washboard road. The Monument has visitor centers at Big Water, Kanab, Cannonville, and an Interagency Visitor Center in the town of Escalante.

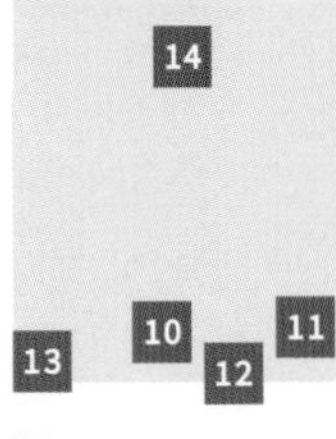

10 Kodachrome Basin State Park

Cannonville, UT 84718; 435-679-8562
stateparks.utah.gov/parks/kodachrome-basin

This beautiful state park sits on the "backside" of Bryce Canyon National Park and includes many of the same iconic red rock hoodoos and spires, without the crowds of a National Park! The unusual name comes from a 1948 National Geographic Expedition that was inspired by the contrast of colors in this region. It is also located right off Utah Scenic Byway 12, one of the most scenic drives in the state. If you're short on time, the Angel's Palace trail is just 1.5 miles with excellent views of Kodachrome Basin and Bryce Canyon. The park also has three campgrounds, horseback riding tours, mountain bike trails, and a disc golf course.

11 Natural Bridges National Monument

San Juan County, UT; 435-692-1234
nps.gov/nabr/index.htm

For great hikes to natural bridges, without the crowds of the National Parks, this national monument 1 hour west of Blanding is perfect. The remote location keeps the crowds at a minimum, and most visitors seem to head for the scenic overlooks, ignoring the hikes below the rim. The monument includes three natural bridges and Ancient Puebloan ruins hidden below a cliff overhang. The Monument has a small museum and gift shop, as well as several scenic overlooks along the one-way 9-mile loop road. For an up-close view of the bridges and the ruins, there are several hiking trails, including one 8.6-mile trail connecting all of the highlights.

12 Rainbow Bridge National Monument

Forbidding Canyon, Lake Powell, UT, 84533; 928-608-6200
nps.gov/rabr

Often hailed as the largest natural bridge in the world, this is a sacred spot to the indigenous people who have lived here for centuries. As such, it's not easy to reach. You can hike in from the Navajo Nation. However, it's 18 miles and you'll need a permit.

The other option is to take a boat tour or rent a small craft from Wahweap Marina on Lake Powell. The length (and availability) of the tour varies based on water levels but generally takes the better part of a full day. Given the crowds of the southwest these days, it's absolutely worth the extra effort to see this 290-foot tall bridge and practically have the place to yourself.

13 Snow Canyon State Park

1002 Snow Canyon Drive, Ivins, UT 84738; 435-628-2255
stateparks.utah.gov/parks/snow-canyon/discover

For fantastic scenery without the crowds of nearby National Parks, the state park near St. George is a hidden gem! With more than 7,000 acres, the landscape includes lava flows and sandstone arches and cliffs. The Johnson Canyon trail is only 2 miles round-trip to a 200-foot arch and is only open from mid-September through March. The Petrified Sand Dunes are a great spot to experience a Southwest sunset. For climbers, there are more than 170 designated climbing routes in the park. In addition to several picnic shelters and restrooms, there is also a campground with water, electric hookups, and showers.

14 Timpanogos Cave National Monument

2038 Alpine Loop Road, American Fork, UT 84003; 801-756-5239
nps.gov/tica/index.htm

Less than 1 hour from Salt Lake City, this national monument is a great day trip from the capital, but you must plan ahead before you visit. For starters, you have to be able to hike 1.5 miles nearly straight uphill, as the caves are set high above the canyon floor. The trail is paved, but steep. You also need to purchase cave tour tickets online; your ticket time will be 90 minutes before your cave tour time, which should be sufficient to hike up. (There are restrooms at the top near the cave.) Once your tour begins, you will visit three distinct caves that were each discovered at different points in time. Inside, you'll see amazing samples of stalactites, stalagmites, columns, draperies, and more. Tours are offered Memorial Day through Labor Day and closed in the winter months.

Arches National Park

UTAH HAS FIVE NATIONAL PARKS, collectively known as "the Mighty Five." Highlighting the best of canyon country, these five parks are often the first (and sometimes only) Utah experience many travelers have. A visit to any of these parks presents a fascinating lesson in geology, anthropology, and history. Strategically located throughout Southern Utah, many visitors plan a road trip incorporating several of these parks. While the parks offer grand viewpoints and scenic drives, there is much to be explored beyond the visitor centers and overlook parking lots. Pack your best hiking boots and lots of water and be prepared to "hit the trail!"

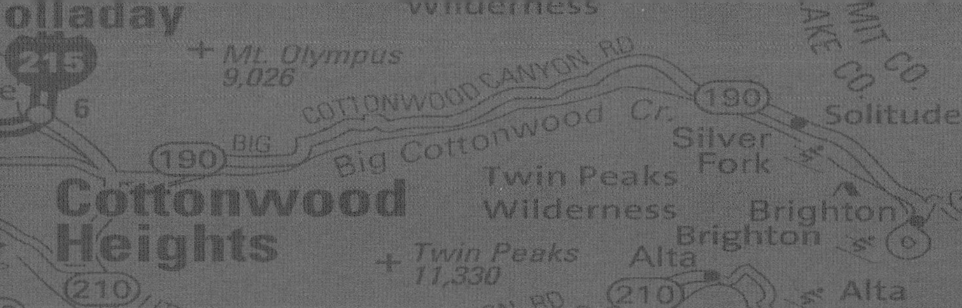

NATIONAL PARKS

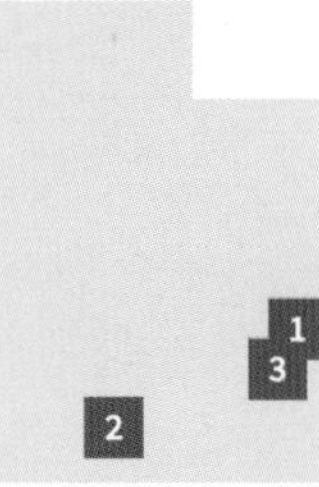

1 Arches National Park

Moab, UT 84532; 435-719-2299
nps.gov/arch/

Although Arches is one of the smaller National Parks in Utah, it packs a lot of scenery into a relatively small space. With more than 2,000 natural arches and bridges, this park is full of surprises around every corner. With many of the top attractions easily accessible along short hiking trails, the trailheads and parking lots at Arches fill up quickly. The park is currently exploring ways to reduce crowds, including timed ticket entry during the busiest months. It's critical to plan ahead and check if reservations are required, especially if traveling during peak season. If you can snag a campsite at Devils Garden Campground, you'll have first access to all the trailheads in the morning! Start your visit with a scenic drive along the main park road, stopping at iconic spots like The Windows, Double Arch, and Balanced Rock. When it comes to iconic hikes at Arches National Park, don't miss out on these three:

- **Devils Garden Trail**—a 7.8-mile loop hike featuring eight arches. Even if you can only hike a couple of miles in, you'll still see some great arches and scenery. As one of the longer trails in Arches National Park, the further you go, the fewer people you will see.
- **Fiery Furnace**—a maze of sandstone canyons; I highly recommend going on a ranger-led tour as it's so easy to get lost in here, and you can learn a lot from the rangers. If you decide to go on your own, you'll need a permit and top-notch navigational skills.
- **Delicate Arch**—This is the most recognizable arch in the park; it's even on our license plates! There are shorter hikes to some nice viewpoints; if you want to hike all the way to the arch, it's 3 miles round-trip, with some cool petroglyphs along the way.

2 Bryce Canyon National Park

Bryce, UT 84764; 435-834-5322
nps.gpv/brca/

At an elevation of nearly 8,000 feet above sea level, the cool, crisp air of Bryce Canyon is a welcome relief from the heat of southern Utah. Visually, this is one of the most stunning national parks in the country. The alien landscape is unlike anything you'll see anywhere else as Bryce Canyon has the largest concentration of hoodoos in the world. Thousands of red and white sandstone hoodoos, spires, and pinnacles fill the canyon as far as the eye can see. As Utah's smallest national park, the scenery at Bryce Canyon is accessible to everyone. A shuttle bus runs along the canyon rim, dropping visitors at various viewpoints along the way. Most of the best viewpoints are accessible and paved, so plan to stop at each of them. If you're up for a hike below the canyon rim, these are some of the best hikes at Bryce Canyon National Park:

- **Navajo Loop Trail** starts at the Wall Street section, a steep series of switchbacks that are better to hike down than up!
- **Queen's Garden Trail** is a great stroll along the canyon floor, with close-up views of rock formations and a gentler incline back to the rim.
- **Combine Navajo Loop Trail and Queen's Garden** trails for a great point to point hike, using the park shuttle to connect the two trailheads.

3 Canyonlands National Park

Moab, UT 84532; 435-719-2313
nps.gov/cany/

Utah's largest national park is so big that it's split into three distinct units. The Island in the Sky unit is in the northern part of the park near Moab and is bordered by the Colorado and Green Rivers. The Needles district makes up the southeast part of the park, while the Maze district covers the southwest part of Canyonlands.

Island in the Sky is the most popular area for day trips, as there is a 34-mile round-trip scenic drive along the top of the mesa, with several scenic overlooks along the way. If you are short on time, spend it on the scenic loop to get the most bang for your buck. The **Needles District** offers dramatic viewpoints and scenic overlooks as well, albeit a bit more off the beaten path, as it's 75 miles from Moab. **The Maze** is very remote and requires a four-wheel-drive to access any of the unpaved roads in this section.

In my opinion, this park is best seen from the backcountry. Consider a Jeep tour or whitewater rafting excursion to really get into the heart of Canyonlands.

4 Capitol Reef National Park

Torrey, UT 84775; 435-425-3791
nps.gov/care/

Utah's least-visited national park is far off the beaten path but offers a lot to see and do for those willing to make the trek. While the main attractions of Capitol Reef are the geologic features formed by the 100-mile Waterpocket Fold, there are also interesting archeological and anthropological attractions as well. Interestingly, the name Capitol Reef does not refer to an ancient underwater reef, but more of an obstruction in the path of travelers; and the Capitol comes from the white sandstone domes that were thought to resemble the Capitol in Washington, D.C. The park follows the Waterpocket Fold from north to south, with most of the main attractions centered along UT 24 in the north. If you have four-wheel drive, a lot more of the park will be accessible to you; however, these are the top things I recommend for a day trip to Capitol Reef National Park:

- Hire a Jeep tour through **Cathedral Valley** in the northern part of the park. Let someone else do the driving, while you enjoy spectacular sites such as the **Temple of the Sun, Temple of the Moon,** and the **Gypsum Sinkhole**.
- Take the short hike to **Hickman Bridge**; the trail to this natural bridge is only 2 miles round-trip, but it does start out fairly steep. Well worth the effort!
- Visit the **Gifford House** in Fruita, and learn about the Latter-day Saints settlers who planted fruit trees here. You can also pick-your-own fruit, depending on what is in season.
- From Fruita, take the scenic drive south for 8 miles, stopping at viewpoints along the way, including the **Petroglyph Panel** along the main highway near the Visitor Center.

5 Zion National Park

Springdale, UT 84767; 435-772-3256
nps.gov/zion/

Less than 3 hours from Las Vegas, Zion National Park is Utah's most-visited national park. The main attractions are located in scenic Zion Canyon, carved by the Virgin River. The park has implemented a shuttle system, which visitors are required to use most of the year to reduce traffic and congestion. (There's also a shuttle that runs through the gateway town of Springdale, so you don't even need to drive to the park.) The park shuttle stops at nine key points along the way, delivering hikers to trailheads and allowing others to simply enjoy the scenery from the comfort of an air-conditioned bus and learn about the area on the narrated tour. The Kolob Canyons section in the northern part of the park is less-visited and home to some great hikes. Zion National Park is home to a couple of quintessential hikes, but I recommend tackling these in the off-season or getting up before sunrise to beat the crowds.

- **Angel's Landing Hike**—This hike is often listed as one of the world's most dangerous hikes, thanks to sheer cliffs dropping off both sides of the trail. The hike is 5 miles round-trip, with spectacular views from the summit. Even if you opt out of the final half-mile section with chains, this is still a great hike, especially the switchbacks known as "Walters Wiggles." As of April 2022, this hike will require a permit that can be obtained through a lottery. Obviously, prepare appropriately and use caution if you undertake this hike.
- **Virgin Rivers Narrows**—This hike offers a great opportunity to experience a slot canyon. For casual hikers, I recommend hiking "bottom-up" from the Temple of Sinawava shuttle stop. Top-down, this is a technical, overnight hike. You'll be walking in the water, so bring a hiking stick. For the best experience, rent wetsuits and boots in town and do this hike in the winter; you may have the canyon all to yourself! (Please check first at the ranger station for the latest updates; flash flooding is a serious and dangerous possibility in slot canyons, as well as possible bacteria in the water that can be dangerous.)

Take in Ballet at Ballet West in Salt Lake City.

WHILE SALT LAKE CITY and the surrounding suburbs are home to the majority of fine arts and performances in Utah, there are art and culture to be had in every corner of the state. From sculpture gardens to contemporary art and performing arts, this is a sampling of some of the work that Utah artists are producing.

THE ARTS

1 Ballet West

50 W 2300 South, Salt Lake City, UT 84101; 801-869-6900
balletwest.org

Entertaining Utah audiences since 1963, Ballet West is led by Adam Sklute, an alumnus of the Joffrey Ballet. With 40 company members, Ballet West has toured the world several times and is often hailed as one of the country's leading dance companies. The season kicks off in October with classics such as *Dracula, The Nutcracker,* and *Romeo and Juliet*. Ballet West also holds an annual performance in Park City, as well as *Ballet West in the Garden*, held at the beautiful amphitheater at Red Butte Gardens. The Ballet West Academy offers pure classical ballet training at campuses in Salt Lake City, Thanksgiving Point, and Park City.

2 Chase Home Museum of Utah Folk Arts

Liberty Park: S Constitution Drive E, Salt Lake City, UT 84105; 801-533-5760
artsandmuseums.utah.gov/chase-home-museum

This is a fun little free museum in Salt Lake City's Liberty Park. This museum is unique in that it is the only museum in the United States that holds a state-owned collection of folk art. The home itself is also part of the museum, as it was built in the early 1850s by a Mormon pioneer, along with a flour mill in the center of a farm that is now Liberty Park. The museum collection includes three permanent exhibitions and one rotating exhibit. One room features American Indian folk art, while another has quilts made by Utahns, and another has a multicultural exhibit showcasing art from Utah's wide variety of cultures.

3 Lyric Repertory Company

28 W Center Street, Logan, UT 84321; 435-797-8022
usu.edu/lyricrep

For more than 50 years, this northern Utah repertory company has been producing musicals, mysteries, comedies, and dramas. Actors from all over the country arrive in Logan each summer to participate in world-class stage productions. From mid-June through early

August, performances and post-performance discussions take place at Utah State University's Morgan Theatre or the Caine Lyric Theatre in downtown Logan.

4 Nora Eccles Harrison Museum of Art

650 N 1100 E, Logan, UT 84322; 435-797-0163
artmuseum.usu.edu

The Eccles family is a name you'll see throughout Utah, as David Eccles was the first multi-millionaire in Utah. Nora Eccles was a philanthropist and potter, whose own works are featured in the vessel collection of the museum. This free art museum at Utah State University features an impressive collection of both modern and contemporary art. With a focus on American art, collections include "Women, Surrealism, and Abstraction" as well as "African American Art, Social Justice, and Identity." Outside, you can explore more than 30 sculptures and statues along the USU Sculpture Walk. The museum also has a mobile art truck, community art days, a museum store, and Noni's Cafe.

5 Southern Utah University Art & Sculpture Stroll

Southern Utah University Campus, 13 S 300 W, Cedar City, UT 84720; 435-586-7700
suu.edu/blog/images/suusculpturebrochure-map.pdf

This was my favorite art experience in Utah! Before setting out, download a map so you can follow along and not miss any of the amazing sculptures on this self-guided art tour. You'll also get a look at the replica Globe theater that is used for the annual Shakespeare festival in Cedar City. There's a Shakespeare character garden, a fountain, a bell tower, and tons of other cool sculptures ranging from classical art to modern. In the southwest corner, the Centurium is a cool monument to historical men and women who are admired for their intellectual contributions to society. Aristotle, Marie Curie, Albert Einstein, and Isaac Newton are just a few of those honored. The entire tour can take about 45 minutes, and free parking is available in the large lot on University Boulevard.

6 Utah Museum of Contemporary Art

20 S W Temple, Salt Lake City, UT 84101; 801-328-4201
utahmoca.org

This downtown Salt Lake museum has undergone many revisions, from the Salt Lake Art Center to the UMOCA that we have today. In 2011, it was rebranded as the contemporary art museum and 10 years later, UMOCA continues to bring modern and contemporary

7, 8

art to Salt Lake locals and visitors alike. Rotating exhibits fill six unique galleries, featuring local, national, and international artists. Exhibits include painting, sculpture, photography, and mixed media pieces. Free family art classes are held every Saturday. Admission to UMOCA is free, although a donation is suggested.

7 Utah Museum of Fine Arts

410 Campus Center Drive, Salt Lake City, UT 84112; 801-581-7332
umfa.utah.edu

Located on the University of Utah campus, this is the largest art museum in the Intermountain West. Holding more than 20,000 pieces in the collection, this museum can easily be an all-day excursion for art lovers. For those with a more casual appreciation of art, you're sure to find something to pique your interest. The collections range from painting, sculpture, photography, and mixed media from artists around the world. The museum also contains a Museum Store and Museum Cafe. Admission is free on the first Wednesday and third Saturday of each month.

8 Utah Symphony | Utah Opera

123 W S Temple, Salt Lake City, UT 84101; 801-533-6683
utahsymphony.org

For performing arts in Utah, it doesn't get much better than this world-class symphony and opera in Salt Lake City. The Utah Symphony is one of the best orchestras in the West and offers more than 70 annual live performances at Abravanel Hall. The Utah Symphony also hosts a hugely popular summer concert series at the Deer Valley Amphitheater in Park City. The Opera hosts four productions each season in the newly-renovated Capitol Theater.

A number of sites across the state offer hands-on art classes

Fantasy Canyon

THESE UTAH ROADSIDE ATTRACTIONS include all things that defy a specific category. From art installations in the desert to alien landscapes, these spots are a great place to stretch your legs while exploring Utah.

ROADSIDE ATTRACTIONS

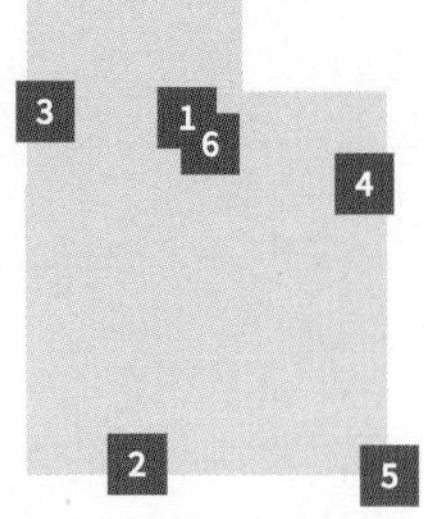

1 Allen Park

1328 E Allen Park Drive, Salt Lake City, UT 84105; 801-514-2681
slc.gov/parks/allenpark

Tucked away in Salt Lake's Sugarhouse Neighborhood, Allen Park is a fun destination for an afternoon stroll. The property along Emigration Creek was originally owned by local doctor George Allen, who created a bird sanctuary on the grounds. The eccentric landowner created several mosaic art pieces around the property, as well as a village of unique duplex and log cabin homes that were inhabited until 2019. Today, the property is a city park where visitors can see the unique homes and pieces of art installed throughout. There is no parking on-site currently.

2 Best Friends Animal Society

5001 Angel Canyon Road, Kanab, UT 84741; 435-644-5000
bestfriends.org

Just 5 miles north of Kanab, this animal sanctuary is a must-see for any animal lover traveling near Kanab. The sanctuary is semi-famous as they took in many dogs from a recent dog-fighting scandal and dogs from Hurricane Katrina, and they were also featured in the TV show *Dogtown*. Best Friends has a goal to end kill shelters by 2025, and you can help by volunteering or scheduling a visit. They have more than 4,000 acres of beautiful southern Utah land and individual sanctuaries for everything from horses to rabbits and guinea pigs. On any given day, there are more than 1,000 animals waiting here for adoption. I visited the Bunny House and had a guided tour of the luxury facilities that include indoor/outdoor space with heated floors! The sanctuary also has on-site camping and lodging that is pet-friendly, of course!

3 Bonneville Salt Flats

I-80 east of Wendover, UT; 801-977-4300
blm.gov/visit/bonneville-salt-flats

The world-famous Bonneville Salt Flats cover 30,000 acres of western Utah, where the ancient Lake Bonneville receded. There is white salt as far as the eye can see, which is pretty cool and not something you can see in many other places. The salt flats are best seen from the rest area 10 miles east of Wendover. You can actually drive your car out on the salt flats here or at the next exit marked Bonneville Salt Flats Speedway. The Speedway road dead-ends, and you can drive out onto the flats. This is where the "measured mile" is located. The world land-speed record was first set here in 1935 at 300 mph, and the location continues to be a popular spot for pushing the limits of automobile speeds.

4 Fantasy Canyon

25 miles southeast of Vernal, UT; 435-781-4400
blm.gov/visit/fantasy-canyon

The remote location of this Bureau of Land Management-managed feature means you might just have the place all to yourself. Fantasy Canyon is a 10-acre site surrounded by private oil corporation land. You'll have little idea of what's ahead, based on the surrounding land. Follow a trail from the parking lot, and you're immediately immersed in bizarre sandstone sculptures. It's hard to even imagine how these formations came to be and how they survive today. There's an official trail through the canyon, but you can also just wander in and out of various coves and dead ends. Interpretive signs are placed throughout to help explain this "fantasy" formation. As long as the approaching dirt road is dry, it is suitable for passenger cars.

5 Four Corners Monument

597 NM 597, Teec Nos Pos, AZ 86514; 928-206-2540
navajonationparks.org/tribal-parks/four-corners-monument

Not far from Monument Valley, the Four Corners Monument is the only place in the United States where four states intersect at one point. Using both hands and feet, you can technically be in four states at the same time. Four Corners is on Navajo land, and the Navajos operate a small gift shop and visitor center on-site. Sure, it's a bit gimmicky, but if it's not too far out of the way, it's worth a quick stop for the photo opportunity.

6 Ice Castles

2002 Soldier Hollow Lane, Midway, UT 84049;
icecastles.com/utah

Ice Castles is a company founded in 2011. As you might expect, they create ice castle destinations, a magical winter experience. If you're lucky enough to be near one of only five locations in the United States, you should visit. The Utah Ice Castles are located in Midway, in the Wasatch Mountains near Salt Lake City. Explore caves and caverns, fountains, and sculptures, all made out of ice. Colorful lights add to the magical atmosphere, as the castles continuously change colors. There are also slides for the kids and a snack stand with hot drinks and warm food.

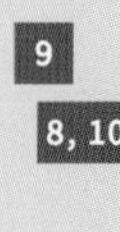

The ground is covered in crushed ice and snow, so wear good snow boots and bring a sled instead of a stroller to pull the kids. Buy your tickets at least a week in advance, as they sell out quickly! Opening and closing dates are weather-dependent, opening in late December or early January and closing usually in late February. Sign up for email updates so you can get tickets when they are about to open.

7 Pando Aspen Forest

Fishlake National Forest, 115 E 900 N, Richfield, UT 84701; 435-896-9233
fs.usda.gov/detail/fishlake/home

When I was driving along Scenic Byway 12, I drove through the largest aspen forest I'd ever seen. It went on forever, which prompted me to research whether it was the largest ever. Turns out, that aspen forest is not the largest, but Utah is home to the largest aspen forest in the world. Covering more than 100 acres and an estimated 40,000 individual trees, this aspen stand is believed to be one of the world's largest living organisms. (A "humongous fungus" in Oregon is its main competition.) Aspen stands share a root system, making them one connected organism. The name Pando is Latin for "I spread" due to the widespread acreage of this unique aspen forest. I can't imagine a more beautiful place to see fall colors.

8 Saltair

12408 W Saltair Drive, Magna, UT 84044; 801-250-6205
thesaltair.com

As you drive along the southern shore of the Great Salt Lake, a Moorish palace appears in the distance. This is the Great Saltair, also known as the SaltAir Resort and now the SaltAir Pavilion. When the railroad was gaining popularity in the Salt Lake Valley in the 1870s, several resorts began to pop up around the lake. Saltair Pavilion was completed in 1893 and was called the "Coney Island of the West." Two iterations burned down, while another was flooded. These factors, along with an increase in auto traffic, and the stock market crash of the '20s led to the demise of the resort. It has been repurposed many times over the years and today remains open occasionally as a concert venue and event space. You can park near the building and walk around; it's shocking to see how far the water has receded!

Spiral Jetty

9 Spiral Jetty

Great Salt Lake at Rozel Point, Corinne, UT 84307; 212-989-5566
diaart.org/visit/visit-our-locations-sites/robert-smithson-spiral-jetty

Texas has Prada Marfa, and Utah has the Spiral Jetty. Set in a remote location along the northeast shore of the Great Salt Lake, this piece of Land Art was installed by American artist Robert Smithson in 1970. From the northern Utah town of Brigham City, it is a 1-hour drive west, and the last 16 miles are along a washboard gravel road. It is accessible for passenger cars and well worth the jarring, slow drive out to see this unique art installation. In addition to admiring this work of art, you can also walk out to the Great Salt Lake. It's fun to explore the salt deposits left behind and see how the lake here is pink from bacteria and crystallized salt deposits. The landscape is breathtaking, and the art adds to the funky atmosphere. Stop at the Golden Spike National Historic Site en route for a map and driving directions to the Spiral Jetty.

10 The *Up* House

13218 S Herriman Rose Boulevard, Herriman, UT 84096
therealuphouse.com

This private home is an exact replica of the Fredricksen house in the Pixar movie *Up*. Located in a suburban development of beige and gray homes, you can't miss this colorful house that sits on the corner across from a park. It is a private home in a neighborhood teeming with children, so keep this in mind and drive carefully while respecting the privacy of the homeowners. The inside and backyard also have iconic mementos from the movie, including furniture and artwork. The family occasionally offers photo shoots around the house, which you can book through their website.

Nebo Loop National Scenic Byway

THE DIVERSE LANDSCAPES OF UTAH are perfect for road trips. From high mountain passes through alpine scenery to wide-open drives through the desert, I've yet to find a drive in Utah that I didn't love. No matter which corner of the state, there's a scenic drive nearby. While these are all accessible in a passenger car, not all of them are for the faint of heart! Amazing views sometimes come with steep drop-offs, and if it's rained recently, be sure to check conditions before setting out. Many of the alpine drives are closed in the winter months, so check the UDOT website before setting out, as a heavy snow year could close the roads through June.

SCENIC DRIVES

1 Alpine Loop Scenic Byway

UT 92 from Wildwood to Cedar Hills

This is a beautiful drive with an abundance of alpine scenery. Starting in Provo Canyon, the route circles the base of Mount Timpanogos, one of the most picturesque peaks in Utah. The road is free to drive, but if you want to park along the way, you'll need to purchase an access pass, which is good for this route, as well as the Mirror Lake Highway. Recommended stops include Sundance Mountain Resort, Stewart Falls, Cascade Springs, and the Timpanogos Cave National Monument. The Alpine Loop is typically open from late May through early October and is not recommended for vehicles longer than 30 feet.

2 Guardsman Pass

UT 224 from Park City to Brighton Resort

Each spring, Park City locals anxiously await the opening of Guardsman Pass. The route climbs out of Park City's Old Town, past the villages of Deer Valley before topping out at 9,700 feet. As you descend into Big Cottonwood Canyon, where Brighton and Solitude ski resorts are located. Bloods Lake is a popular hike near the summit. After the pass, you can go left into Wasatch Mountain State Park in Midway or go right to Brighton Resort and eventually Salt Lake City. There are some great hikes near Brighton, including the Silver Lake boardwalk, which is just under 1 mile. There are no dogs allowed in Big Cottonwood Canyon. The road is typically open from late May through October and is a great place for fall color as there are several aspen stands near the summit.

3 Logan Canyon Scenic Byway

US 89 from Logan to Garden City

Beautiful in every season, the Logan Canyon Scenic Byway leaves the agricultural hub of Cache Valley and climbs along the Bear River for 16 miles to Garden City and Bear Lake. Open year-round, this scenic route passes Beaver Mountain Ski Area as well as Beaver Creek Lodge, a popular snowmobile and ATV lodge. In the summer, the highway sees a lot of travelers and boats headed to beautiful Bear Lake. Fall color is amazing, and in winter, the well-maintained highway provides easy access to winter adventures.

4 Mirror Lake Scenic Byway

UT 150 from Kamas to Wyoming

The Mirror Lake Highway is my favorite local scenic drive, and the best way to beat the heat in the summer months. From the ranching town of Kamas, UT 150 climbs to 10,687 feet at Bald Mountain Pass, before descending to Mirror Lake and eventually continuing on to the Utah-Wyoming border. Along the way, you'll pass dozens of lakes, campgrounds, and trailheads. Make sure to stop at the Provo River Falls to stretch your legs, and at the overlook just past Bald Mountain. When you reach Mirror Lake campground, there's a nice 1.5-mile trail around the lake as well as a boat launch for canoes and kayaks. The road is typically open from late May through October. Bring cash for the self-service pay stations.

5 Moki Dugway

UT 261 from Natural Bridges National Monument to Valley of the Gods

The Moki Dugway is one of my favorite scenic drives in Utah. From the high desert of Cedar Mesa to the valley floor below, the well-graded dirt road drops quickly and offers fantastic views along the way. The 34-mile road is a nice shortcut between Bears Ears National Monument and Monument Valley. I stumbled on this one accidentally the first time, not wanting to backtrack to the highway. There are definitely some drop-offs on this route, and it can be intimidating from afar. My mother refused to let me take this road when she was along for the ride, so beware if anyone has a fear of heights. However, the road itself is fine (in good weather) for a passenger car as long as you're cautious, and I can't recall a better example of literally driving through the earth's geologic record as you step gradually down to the valley floor.

6 Nebo Loop Scenic Byway

FR 015 from Nephi to Payson

For stunning alpine scenery at every turn, this 32-mile scenic route takes the cake. Even if you're just driving through Utah, this route parallels I-15 and makes for a great detour from the interstate. The narrow road is fully paved, with several stops and pull-outs along the way; there are no guardrails. The route circles Mount Nebo, which is the highest point in the Wasatch Mountains at 11,928 feet. Much of the byway is also open cattle range, so make sure you are sticking to

the 30 mph speed limit, as cows are frequently out and about. Each corner brings a new view; the wildflowers in summer are amazing, and the fall color is equally beautiful. In addition to trailheads and hikes, there are several campgrounds and day-use areas at some of the lakes. Topping out at 9,345 feet in elevation, the Nebo Loop is closed in winter.

7 Utah Scenic Byway 12

UT 12 from Bryce Canyon City to Torrey

Scenic Byway 12 is frequently rated as one of the most scenic drives in the United States. The route stretches 124 miles and reaches up to 9,636 feet above sea level. It passes by Bryce Canyon National Park, Kodachrome Basin State Park, Grand Staircase Escalante National Monument, Escalante Petrified Forest State Park, and one of the largest aspen forests I've ever seen, before dropping back into the desert near Torrey and Capitol Reef National Park. The Hogback section famously has steep drop-offs on both sides, but the scenery is so spectacular, you don't even notice! This route has it all: dramatic mountain views, arches, slot canyons, waterfalls, and artsy desert towns. Be sure to allow plenty of time to soak it all in.

8 Valley of the Gods

Valley of the Gods Road, Mexican Hat

If you are coming down the Moki Dugway, the 17-mile gravel detour through Valley of the Gods is totally worth it. People have called this a "miniature Monument Valley," which gives you an idea of what it looks like, but you'll see far fewer travelers on this route. Unlike Monument Valley, it is free to visit the Valley of the Gods, and dispersed camping is allowed. It's also fine for passenger cars in good weather. From the southern terminus of the route, Goosenecks State Park is less than 15 minutes away.

Scenic Byway 12; Grand Staircase Esalante National Monument

Red Pine Gondola at Park City Mountain Resort

UTAH CLAIMS TO HAVE the "Greatest Snow on Earth." It's been trademarked, and it's on the license plates, so take it as a fact. Big Cottonwood and Little Cottonwood Canyons average over 550 inches of snow annually, making them two of the snowiest places in the world. That's why you'll find 14 ski resorts in Utah, 10 of them within an hours' drive from the capital city and international airport. Utah ski resorts have something for every type of skier and snowboarder. If you want to sample them all as I did, you can buy a Yeti Pass, which gives you one ski day at each of Utah's 14 ski resorts! Come summer, these resorts make great hiking and biking destinations.

SKI RESORTS

Navajo Express Lift at Brian Head Resort

2, 5

1, 4

3

1 Alta Ski Area

UT 210 Alta, UT 84092; 801-359-1078
alta.com/

Alta is one of just three resorts in the United States that does not allow snowboards, which makes it a local favorite for old-school skiers. With 55 percent of the terrain designated as advanced, skiing at Alta is definitely geared toward more-advanced skiers. Services are split between Albion base and the Wildcat base, with a transfer tow and Nordic track between the two. Expert skiers can utilize a series of traverses to access additional terrain beyond the lifts, as well as a few black diamond runs connecting Alta with Snowbird. Alta features five on-site lodges, and there are many private chalet and condo rentals nearby.

- **Number of Runs:** 116
- **Terrain:** Beginner, 15%; Intermediate, 30%; Advanced, 55%

2 Beaver Mountain Ski Resort

12400 E 12900 N, Logan, UT 84028; 435-946-3610
skithebeav.com

Located in beautiful Logan Canyon, Beaver Mountain Ski Resort has been family-owned and operated since 1939, making it the oldest continuously-owned family ski resort in the United States. For skiers accustomed to the glitz and glamour of big corporate resorts, Beaver Mountain is a refreshingly laid-back and affordable resort with everything you need for an exciting day on the slopes. You're likely to meet one or more members of the Seeholzer family during your visit, as the owners are very involved in the day-to-day operations. There is no man-made snow at Beaver Mountain; it's all Mother Nature, so the season open and close are weather dependent, but the location in the Bear River Range is not lacking for snow. The parking lot is practically famous for tailgating, but the food at the Beaver Mountain Grill is too tasty (and affordable!) to pass up. Lodging is available nearby at Bear Lake and Garden City, or in Logan.

- **Number of Runs:** 48
- **Terrain:** Beginner, 35%; Intermediate, 40%; Advanced, 25%

3 Brian Head Ski Resort

329 UT 143, Brian Head, UT 84719; (435) 677-2035
brianhead.com/

Utah's southernmost ski resort is located near the red rock hoodoos of Cedar Break National Monument, and just 1 hour from Bryce Canyon National Park. Don't let the latitude fool you; Brian Head has a higher base elevation than any other Utah ski resort, meaning they have great snow and are often open later than many of the other Utah resorts. There is plenty of terrain for all types of skiers, as well as several snow tubing lanes accessed by a magic carpet. Two base areas offer skier services and dining, with a free shuttle bus running between the two. The village of Brian Head has additional lodging and dining options, while nearby towns of Beaver and Cedar City are each about 45 minutes away.

- **Number of Runs:** 71
- **Terrain:** Beginner, 30%; Intermediate, 35%; Advanced, 35%

4 Brighton Resort

8302 S Brighton Loop Road, Brighton, UT 84121; (801) 532-4731
brightonresort.com/

At the top of Big Cottonwood Canyon, Brighton remains delightfully quaint and is one of my favorite summer hiking destinations. It also seems to be the most beginner-friendly of the four Cottonwood Canyons ski resorts. Affordable lift tickets and night skiing make this a popular resort for Salt Lake City families when choosing a ski school. The base area includes several dining choices, as well as the Brighton Lodge. In the summer, Brighton is just minutes from Park City via Guardsman Pass, one of the best scenic drives in the area. The Brighton Lodge offers on-site lodging, while nearby Solitude Village offers many more options.

- **Number of Runs:** 66
- **Terrain:** Beginner, 23%; Intermediate, 39%; Advanced, 38%

5 Cherry Peak Resort

3200 E 11000 N, Richmond, UT 84333; 435-200-5050
skicpr.com/

One of Utah's newest ski resorts, Cherry Peak is a family adventure destination in Northern Utah. With affordable lift tickets and a tubing hill, Cherry Peak has something for everyone. Primarily an evening destination, Cherry Peak is only open for daytime skiing on Friday, Saturday, Sunday, and select bonus days each month. The day lodge

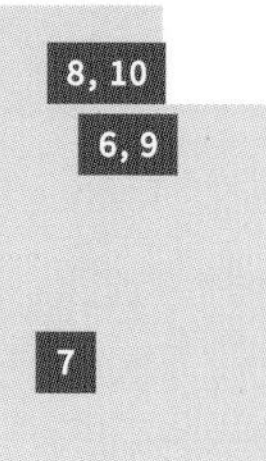

includes the Peak Grill, rental shop, and ski school. For overnight lodging, Logan is just 30 minutes away.

- **Number of Runs:** 20
- **Terrain:** Beginner, 30%; Intermediate, 45%; Advanced, 25%

6 Deer Valley Resort

2250 Deer Valley Drive S, Park City, UT 84060; (435) 649-1000
deervalley.com/

One of Utah's most exclusive ski resorts, Deer Valley has been voted best in North America by *SKI Magazine* several years running. With peak season lift tickets north of $200 per day, plus five-star lodging and fine dining, Deer Valley is also the most expensive ski resort in Utah. Located just 5 minutes from downtown Park City, Deer Valley is best known for well-groomed runs and a highly-rated ski school. Deer Valley was limiting daily sales long before COVID, making it a favorite for any skier who hates lift lines. For the 2002 Winter Olympics, Deer Valley hosted the freestyle moguls, aerial, and alpine slalom events. Snowboarding events were held elsewhere, as Deer Valley is a ski-only resort.

- **Number of Runs:** 103
- **Terrain:** Beginner, 27%; Intermediate, 41%; Advanced, 32%

7 Eagle Point Resort

150 S W Village Cir, Beaver, UT 84713; (435) 438-3700
eaglepointresort.com/

A family-friendly, scenic ski destination in southwest Utah, Eagle Point is a great spot for beginners looking to improve their skills on easier blue runs. The resort is only open Friday through Sunday, so it's a great weekend getaway in southern Utah. Skier services are split between two base areas; Canyonside Lodge offers access to advanced terrain, while the Skyline Lodge has access to more beginner and intermediate terrain, as well as the terrain parks. For added convenience, a shuttle runs between the two. Liftlines at Eagle Point are nearly non-existent, meaning more time on your skis! Choose from on-site condominium rentals or lodging nearby in Beaver or Cedar City.

- **Number of Runs:** 40
- **Terrain:** Beginner, 21%; Intermediate, 36%; Advanced, 43%

8 Nordic Valley Ski Resort

3567 Nordic Valley Way, Eden, UT 84310; (801) 745-3511
nordicvalley.ski/

One of Utah's smallest ski resorts also happens to have the most terrain for night skiing. This is the only Utah ski resort where all runs are lit for night skiing, not just a select few. Just 25 minutes from downtown Ogden, Nordic Valley is a simple resort with affordable lift tickets and basic amenities. A brand new six-person high-speed chairlift installed in 2020 opens access to another 300 acres of skiable area. The low elevation and beginner-friendly terrain make this a great first stop if you're skiing multiple resorts out of Ogden.

- **Number of Runs:** 23
- **Terrain:** Beginner, 35%; Intermediate, 45%; Advanced, 20%

9 Park City Mountain Resort

1345 Lowell Ave, Park City, UT 84060; (435) 649-8111
parkcitymountain.com/

Park City Mountain hosted four events during the 2002 Winter Olympics and in 2015 combined with the Canyons to create the largest ski resort experience in North America. Start at the Town Lift, which takes you directly from Park City Main Street to the heart of the ski slopes. Throughout the day, you'll ski past several old mining relics, as more than 30 mines once operated within today's resort boundaries. Beginner skiers will love long, easy runs like Home Run, with more than 3.5 miles of easy winding terrain to the resort base. Expert skiers will appreciate access to 13 backcountry bowls and eight terrain parks. On the Canyons side, enjoy more advanced terrain, fewer crowds, and a five-star village surrounded by luxury resorts. Park City's free public bus system makes it easy to get between the two villages and back to your accommodations at the end of the day.

- **Number of Runs:** 348
- **Terrain:** Beginner, 8%; Intermediate, 41%; Advanced, 51%

10 Powder Mountain

6965 E Powder Mountain Road, Eden, UT 84310; (801) 745-3772
powdermountain.com/

Powder Mountain claims to be the largest North American ski resort with the smallest crowds. With the most skiable acres of any ski resort in the United States, this is a hidden gem of skiing

in Utah. What makes Powder Mountain really stand out is that only 3,000 acres are lift-served, leaving the rest for skiers who want to leave the groomed runs behind. This is a great location to try snowcat skiing at affordable prices or take a tour with a backcountry guide. Given the unique terrain at Powder Mountain, there's a shuttle bus system that stops at various points throughout the resort to assist those skiers who've left the lifts behind and carved their own route. Four lodges serve as base areas for the resort, and lodging is available on-site as well as in Ogden, just 20 miles away.

- **Number of Runs:** 154
- **Terrain:** Beginner, 25%; Intermediate, 40%; Advanced, 35%

11 Snowbasin Resort

3925 SnowBasin Road, Huntsville, UT 84317; (801) 620-1000
snowbasin.com/

This Ogden area resort was home to the 2002 Winter Olympic men's and women's downhill, combined, and Super-G events. It's one of the oldest continuously operating ski resorts in the United States, having been in operation since 1939. Luxurious day lodges offer a variety of dining and shopping opportunities. The Needles gondola allows pedestrian traffic in winter and summer, while an additional tram and chairlift allow passengers in the winter, meaning you don't even have to be a skier or snowboarder to enjoy the magnificent scenery of Snowbasin. For lodging, you can find a few inns and vacation homes in nearby Huntsville, or hotels in Ogden, just 30 minutes away.

- **Number of Runs:** 107
- **Terrain:** Beginner, 10%; Intermediate, 60%; Advanced, 30%

12 Snowbird

9385 S. Snowbird Center Drive, Snowbird, UT, 84092; 800-232-9542
snowbird.com/

This resort in Little Cottonwood Canyon is rated one of North America's most-challenging ski resorts. While there is a bit of beginner terrain, Snowbird is a paradise for intermediate-to-advanced skiers, as a lot of skiing is off-piste, or ungroomed. Lucky for green-run skiers such as myself, there's an aerial tram that allows pedestrian traffic, both ways. If you can handle an "easier" blue run, don't miss the chance to ski through North America's only ski tunnel. The Peruvian tunnel takes skiers on a 600-foot magic carpet to Mineral Basin, with ski runs on the other side of Hidden Peak. With flexible open and close dates, ski lifts run well into May, giving Snowbird the longest ski season in Utah. There are several on-site lodging choices, as well as an amazing spa, and the Salt Lake Valley is just 25 minutes away.

- **Number of Runs:** 140
- **Terrain:** Beginner, 27%; Intermediate, 38%; Advanced, 35%

13 Solitude Mountain Resort

12000 Big Cottonwood Canyon Road, Solitude, UT 84121; (801) 534-1400
solitudemountain.com/

This resort in Big Cottonwood Canyon is one of the nearest ski resorts to Salt Lake City. With 90 percent of the terrain designated for intermediate and expert skiers and boarders, this ski resort is not great for beginners. (Beginners should continue up the road to Brighton.) However, Solitude Village is a great destination for those who don't want to commute from Salt Lake City to ski. In addition to the base at Solitude Village, there is also the Moonbeam Base Area, with access to beginner terrain and the Solitude Nordic Center, with a shuttle bus running between the two. For the most adventurous skiers, you can ski over to Brighton resort, knocking out two resorts in one day!

- **Number of Runs:** 82 named runs
- **Terrain:** Beginner, 10%; Intermediate, 40%; Advanced, 50%

14 Sundance Mountain Resort

8841 N. Alpine Loop Road, Sundance, UT 84604; 801-225-4107
sundanceresort.com/

One of my favorite Utah Valley destinations in any season is Sundance Mountain Resort. This Provo Canyon community built by Robert Redford in the 1970s is much more than a ski resort. It's a place where artists can gather, learn, and be inspired. It's also a luxury resort, with adventures such as horseback riding, zip-lining, Nordic skiing, fly fishing, luxury lodging, a spa, and several fantastic restaurants. Ski runs at Sundance offer something for every skill level, including a fun obstacle course of Wild West replicas through which you can ski on the Outlaw Trail. With up-close views of Mount Timpanogos, Sundance tops my list of scenic ski resorts.

- **Number of Runs:** 44
- **Terrain:** Beginner, 35%; Intermediate, 45%; Advanced, 20%

Basketball is ever popular in Utah.

WHILE TEAM SPORTS may not be the first thing that comes to mind when you think of Utah, there are still plenty of sporting events to attend in Utah. Choose from the National Basketball League, Major League Rugby, and Major League Soccer, as well as many minor league teams to follow. Of course, with the University of Utah and Brigham Young University located in Salt Lake City and Provo, college game days are a big draw as well.

SPORTS

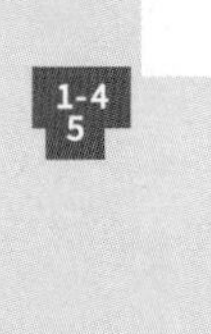

1 Real Salt Lake

Rio Tinto Stadium: 9256 S State Street, Sandy, UT 84070; 844-732-3849
rsl.com

RSL came on the soccer scene in 2004 and soon moved into its home at Rio Tinto Stadium in Sandy. The name is an homage to Real Madrid, one of Europe's biggest soccer teams. Real Salt Lake played 17 regular season matches at home each season and brought home the Major League Soccer Cup in 2009. In 2010-2011, RSL was a runner-up in the International CONCACAF Champions League. A cult following among Salt Lake City locals keeps the stadium full for most home matches, and Rio Tinto also hosts concerts when RSL is away.

2 Salt Lake Bees

Smith's Ballpark: 77 W 1300 S, Salt Lake City, UT 84115; 801-325-2337
milb.com/salt-lake

While having a Major League Baseball team in Utah would be a dream come true, there is beauty in the simplicity of minor league games. Ticket prices and parking are much more amenable than MLB games, meaning families can enjoy a game without mortgaging the house. The Salt Lake Bees are a feeder team for the Los Angeles Angels, so it's also fun to see up-and-coming players before they get called up. The SLC Bees tagline is "The Best View in Baseball," and I can't argue with that!

3 Utah Grizzlies

Maverik Center: 3200 S Decker Lake Drive, West Valley City, UT 84119; 801-988-8000
utahgrizzlies.com

Thankfully, the only grizzlies in Utah are the ones who play hockey at the Maverik Center in West Valley City. The Utah Grizzlies play in the mid-level East Coast Hockey League league and are affiliated with the Colorado Avalanche and the Colorado Eagles teams. With a capacity of more than 12,000 seats, the Grizzlies play more than 20 home games between October and February each season. The Maverik Center famously hosted some of the 2002 Winter Olympic ice hockey games and continues to host concerts and special events when the Grizzlies are off the ice.

4 Utah Jazz

Vivint Arena: 301 S Temple, Salt Lake City, UT 84101; 801-325-2000
nba.com/jazz

You can't beat the frenetic energy and fast pace of a National Basketball Association game, and the Utah Jazz fills the 18,000-seat Vivint Arena nearly every night of their home games. The 1996-1997 Jazz team had the best record in franchise history with big-name players Karl Malone and John Stockton, both of whom have Salt Lake City streets named in their honor. With new owners and a recent playoff run, the team is poised for success in the upcoming seasons. No matter who wins, attending a game at Vivint Arena is a must for sports fans in Salt Lake City. In addition to major concert productions, Vivint Arena hosted figure skating and short-track speedskating events at the 2002 Olympic Winter Games.

5 Utah Warriors

Zions Bank Stadium: 14787 Academy Parkway, Herriman, UT 84096; 800-935-4045
warriorsrugby.com

Major League Rugby is fairly new to the United States, having launched in 2018. The Utah Warriors have been playing matches since 2010. Home matches are played at Zions Bank Stadium in Herriman, a 5,000-seat arena that is also home to the Real Monarchs, a feeder team for Real Salt Lake. The Warriors play an average of eight home games during the regular season, which runs from February through June.

Heber Valley Railroad, Heber City

TRAINS AND PLANES ARE an integral part of Utah's history. The arrival of rail lines hastened the development of Utah communities as pioneers and cowboys rushed to the West. Trains ushered in the era of tourism in the West, and many Utah towns owe their existence to the railways, whether from tourism or mining. The wide-open spaces of the high desert are perfect for aircraft testing, and Utah has long ties to the military and the aviation industry.

TRAINS & PLANES

1, 2

1 ATK Rocket Garden

9160 UT 83, Corinne, UT 84307
northropgrumman.com

If you are planning to visit the Spiral Jetty and the Golden Spike National Historic Site, don't miss this gem in the same area. ATK Thiokol was a major aerospace and defense contractor that used to make the rocket boosters for NASA's space shuttles. Although ATK was acquired by Northrop Grumman in 2017, the ATK Rocket Garden is still in place. It's free to visit and only takes a few minutes to see all of the missiles, test motors, and boosters on display. The scale of the pieces is impressive, and it's a fun experience to walk among these marvels of science.

ATK Rocket Garden in Corinne, Utah

Jupiter Steam Locomotive at Golden Spike National Historic Park

2 Golden Spike National Historic Park

6200 N 22300 W, Corinne, UT 84307; 435-471-2209
nps.gov/gosp/index.htm

On May 10, 1869, the Union Pacific Railway and the Central Pacific Railway met at this spot, connecting Omaha to Sacramento. Thus, the first transcontinental railway was created, to much fanfare and celebration. A telegraph wire was even installed ahead of the ceremony to broadcast the news across the nation. Some even say this was the first national media event. Today, the site is part of the National Park Service and is open for visitors. They have daily steam engine demonstrations in the summer, as well as an annual reenactment of the Golden Spike ceremony. Inside the visitor center, they show a 20-minute orientation film and have many other films available on request. If you have an extra hour, continue down the gravel road to see the Spiral Jetty on the Great Salt Lake.

3 Heber Valley Railroad

450 S 600 W, Heber City, UT 84032; 435-654-5601
hebervalleyrr.org

This railway ferried freight and passengers between Heber City and Provo until 1967. Today, the Heber Valley Railroad, aka the Heber Creeper, is the only scenic railroad tour in Utah. It features several historic railcars and cabooses that have been lovingly restored. Stretching 16 miles through the beautiful Provo Canyon, passengers are treated to amazing views of Mount Timpanogos, Deer Creek Reservoir, the Provo River, Sundance Resort, and Soldier Hollow. There are several tours from which to choose from and seasonal themes that include the Halloween Train and the North Pole Express. Personally, I think fall is the best time to experience this journey when the trees are bursting with color. You also have the option to purchase a combo ticket to include river rafting or zip lining after your train ride.

4 Hill Aerospace Museum

7961 Cottonwood Street, Building 1955, Hill AFB, UT 84056; 801-825-5817
aerospaceutah.org

Located north of Salt Lake City between Ogden and Layton, this free museum has more than 70 aircraft on display. There also are thousands of artifacts depicting the history of aviation of the U.S. Air Force, Hill Air Force Base, and the state of Utah. Spread across 30 acres, there are a dozen planes outdoors, and the rest are housed in two large hangars. Each aircraft has a plaque describing the history of the aircraft and its relevance to Hill Air Force Base. There even is one of LBJ's Air Force One airplanes and a special variant of the iconic Lockheed SR-71 Blackbird surveillance aircraft. Regular airplane talks and tours are scheduled, in addition to robust children's STEM programming.

5 Historic Wendover Airfield Museum

352 E Airport Way, Wendover, UT 84083; 435-665-7724
wendoverairbase.com

Take a step back in time at this historic museum near the Nevada border in western Utah. An Army airbase was established here in

1940 and soon came to play a critical role in World War II. At one time, this was the largest military reserve in the world. Thanks in part to a remote location in the western Utah desert, Wendover was chosen as the place to rehearse atomic weapon delivery. Most heavy bomber crews trained here, including the Enola Gay. The museum is housed in several buildings, including a beautifully restored service club that includes a mess hall, bar, and dance hall. Daily tours are given at 1:30 p.m., starting in the Service Club foyer. Although the airbase closed in 1963, you may still see a few private planes dropping by for a refuel, as this is an active airfield.

6 Ogden Union Station

2501 Wall Ave, Ogden, UT 84401; 801-629-8680
ogdencity.com/1562/Union-Station

Set at the end of Ogden's Historic 25th Street, this beautiful historic transportation hub is full of interesting exhibits. Ogden's Union Station has four museums within. The Utah State Railroad Museum, the John M. Browning Firearms Museum, the Browning–Kimball Classic Car Museum, and the Utah Cowboy Western Heritage Museum are all part of the historical attractions at Union Station. Inside, you'll also find two art galleries and a research library. It's a great place to learn about Utah's history, Ogden's history, and how the railroad fit into the evolution of the state. Don't miss out on the restaurants and shops just outside on Historic 25th Avenue!

7 Tooele Valley Museum and Historical Park

35 N Broadway Street, Tooele, UT 84074; 435-882-2836
tooelevalleymuseum.com

This free museum is a great place to learn about the Tooele Valley and the town of Tooele, which today is best known for the Army Depot formed here in 1942. The smelter is what originally put Tooele on the map, and it was known as the "Smelter City." The museum itself is located in a historic train depot designated as a National Historic Site. The yard features several historic rail cars, including several you can tour. Inside the museum, there are many artifacts about the railroad, the mine of the area, the railroad, and the people who originally settled here. There are also several children's areas to play, as well as a park outside. The museum is closed in winter, opening Memorial Day through September.

Utah State Capitol

LIKE MANY PARTS OF THE "WILD WEST," Utah has a unique collection of historic monuments and buildings dedicated to the pioneers who settled here and the Indigenous people who were here long before. It's hard to separate historic sites in Utah, as many of them tie into the history of Americans Indians who have been here for centuries and the history of The Church of Jesus Christ of Latter-day Saints, which brought the first pioneers to the area. Thus, many historic sites can be interesting to a host of different visitors.

HISTORIC SITES

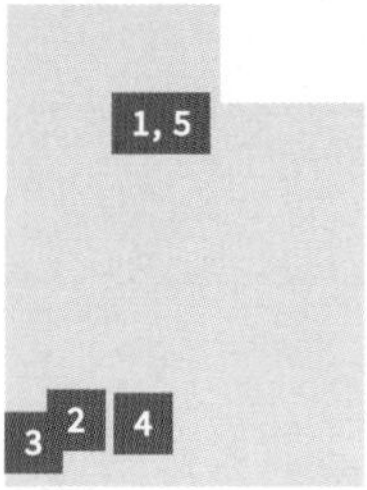

1, 5

3 2 4

1 Daughters of Utah Pioneers Museums

300 N Main Street, Salt Lake City, UT 84103; 801-532-6479
isdup.org/index.php

The International Society Daughters of Utah Pioneers is an organization dedicated to honoring the settlers who founded the state of Utah. They maintain an impressive collection of artifacts, with the largest collection found at the main museum in Salt Lake City, also called the Pioneer Memorial Museum. However, DUP has satellite museums all over both Utah and Idaho. Some of the satellite museums exist inside other buildings, such as the visitor center in Cedar City, while others are open by appointment only. You can learn a lot about pioneer life by taking a quick spin through one of the satellite museums.

2 Frontier Homestead State Park Museum

635 N Main Street, Cedar City, UT 84721; 435-586-9290
stateparks.utah.gov/parks/frontier-homestead/directions/

Set on Cedar City's Main Street, this is a great first stop on your visit to Iron County. Learn how the discovery of iron nearby led to this area being settled by the Mormon pioneers in 1850. Inside the museum, there are several stagecoaches on display, including a Wells Fargo mail coach that you can climb aboard for a photo op. Outside, there are several buildings that have been refurbished to resemble a nineteenth-century homestead. A schoolhouse, garden, sawmill, blast furnace, and a Paiute camp are just a few of the places to learn about the life of early settlers and Utah natives. Hands-on activities include panning for gold and doing the laundry on a washboard. Check the website for special events held throughout the year. Afterward, visit the Old Irontown Ruins, a nearby ghost town where iron was processed.

3 Mountain Meadows Massacre Site

Mountain Meadow Monument Trail, Central, UT

This site marks one of the most brutal events in Utah's history. In September 1857, a group of more than 100 emigrants was passing through what is now southeast Utah en route to California, when

Mormon leaders launched an attack, using local Paiute Indians as cover. When they thought their cover had been blown, they launched a full-out attack disguised as a surrender and spared only young children. While this is a dark part of Utah's history, it's also an important story to be told. The location is somewhat remote but not far from Veyo Pool or the Old Irontown ruins.

4 Ruby's Inn

26 S Main Street, Bryce Canyon City, UT 84764; 866-866-6616
rubysinn.com

Ruby's Inn has been a travel destination before Bryce Canyon was even a national monument. The original Ruby's Inn was established in 1919 by Reuben Syrett, also known as Ruby. He settled his family nearby and began construction on a lodge near the rim of the canyon. While the lodge is now owned by Best Western, it still retains its historic Western atmosphere and still employs several of Ruby's descendants. Whether you stay here or elsewhere when visiting Bryce Canyon National Park, be sure to stop and look around. You can learn a lot just by walking the halls on the first floor. There's also a huge gift shop, grocery store, restaurant, and activities center. The Bryce Canyon shuttle stops right in front, so you can easily explore the park without the hassle of driving and parking.

5 Utah State Capitol

350 State Street, Salt Lake City, UT 84103; 801-538-1800
utahstatecapitol.utah.gov

The stunning Utah State Capitol building sits on a hill overlooking Salt Lake City. It is one of only a few statehouses in the country where all three branches still reside in one building. Originally built in 1916, the Capitol is a magnificent building inside and outside. A major restoration in 2008 added impressive earthquake proofing and restored much of the original artwork and fixtures. The rotunda is surrounded by massive marble columns and beautiful paintings throughout the building depicting the history of Utah. The House of Representatives and Senate sessions are open to the public, and free tours are given several times daily between Monday and Friday. Outside, more than 400 cherry trees bloom each spring, bringing many visitors to stroll along the pathway circling the Capitol. Across the street from the southern entrance, pop into the Utah Office of Tourism for maps, brochures, and souvenirs.

Dented Brick Distillery

IN A STATE KNOWN FOR restrictive liquor laws, there is a surprising number of breweries and distilleries in Utah. Craft brews and mountain biking seem to go hand in hand, so you'll find a ton of local brews in the Moab region. *Note:* Utah grocery stores and convenience stores can sell beer that is up to 5 percent Alcohol By Volume; everything else must be purchased in a store run by the Utah Department of Alcoholic Beverage Control. The stores often have somewhat limited hours, so be sure to plan ahead! Call ahead if you're traveling with children, as many bars and tasting rooms do not allow anyone under the age of 21.

BREWERIES, DISTILLERIES, & WINERIES

1 Utah Ale Trail

Statewide
utahaletrail.com

The number of breweries in Utah has more than doubled in the last 10 years, a testament to the passion of brewers fighting an uphill battle against liquor regulations. Whether you prefer IPA, sour, stout, porter, pilsner, or lager, you'll find a local version at one of more than 40 breweries in Utah. The majority of breweries are located in the Salt Lake Valley along the Wasatch front, but you'll also find a handful in Moab, Vernal, and the St. George area. Not sure what to try? Ask a local, and they'll point you in the right direction. I'm not a big drinker, but so far, I'm digging the hard seltzer from Grid City Beer Works in Salt Lake City.

2 Utah Spirit Trail

Statewide
utahspirittrail.com

The best way to experience Utah's craft distilling culture is to take a self-guided tour on the Spirit Trail. Simply go online to purchase the guide, plan your route, and don't forget to get your guide stamped at each stop. Once you've got all the stamps, you can send in the guide for a trophy and certificate of completion. Along the way, you'll learn a lot about the history of distilling in Utah, as well as the ongoing challenges faced by craft distillers. If you don't have a designated driver, Sprinter van tours can easily be arranged.

Beehive Distilling
The first gin distillery in Utah since 1870; producing two types of gin and vodka
2245 S W Temple, South Salt Lake, UT 84115; 385-259-0252
beehivedistilling.com

Dented Brick Distillery
Best known for Antelope Island Rum; they also make gin, vodka, and whiskey
3100 S Washington Street, South Salt Lake, UT 84115; 801-883-9837
dentedbrick.com

Eight Settlers Distillery
Utah's newest edition to the distillery trail, this distillery focuses on fine food and spirits
7321 Canyon Centre Parkway, Cottonwood Heights, UT 84121; 385900-4315
eightsettlersdistillery.com

Hammer Spring Distillers
Offering gin, vodka, coffee liqueur, and Utah's only distilled potato vodka
3697 W 1987 S, Building 5, Salt Lake City, UT 84104; 801-599-4704
hammerspring.com

High West Distillery

Utah's first legal whiskey producer since 1870, with a ski-in saloon in Park City

27649 Old Lincoln Highway, Wanship, UT 84017; 435-649-8300
highwest.com

The Hive Winery & Spirits Company

Producing countless flavors of wine, hard cider, and mead from local fruits and honey

1220 W Jack D Drive #2, Layton, UT 84041; 801-546-1997
thehivewinery.com

Holystone Distilling

Producing small-batch gin, a grape-based vodka, and absinthe

207 4860 S, Salt Lake City, UT 84107; 503-328-4356
holystonedistilling.com

Ogden's Own Distillery

Best known for their Five Wives vodka; they also make gin, whiskey, and herbal liqueur.

615 W. Stockman Way, Ogden, UT 84401; 801-458-1995
ogdensown.com

Outlaw Distillery

Producing handcrafted whiskey, bourbon, and rum from locally sourced ingredients

552 W 8360 S, Midvale, UT 84070; 801-706-1428
outlawdistillery.com

Silver Reef Distillery

This southern Utah brand is known for Holiday Nog, rum, bourbon, brandy, and a silver vodka

4391 Enterprise Drive, St. George, UT 84790; 435-216-1050
stgeorgebev.com

Sugar House Distillery

Sample Utah's first locally-produced rum at this grain-to-glass production facility

2212 S W Temple #14, Salt Lake City, UT 84115; 801-726-0403
sugarhousedistillery.net

Dented Brick Distillery

3 Utah Wineries

Statewide

While Utah is not necessarily known for wine, there are a few wineries on the scene where you can sample locally produced wines in some amazing locations.

Château LaCaille Winery

Sample red and white wines from grapes grown at the mouth of Cottonwood Canyon

9565 Wasatch Boulevard, Sandy, UT 84092; 801-942-1751
chateaulacaille.com

The Hive Winery & Spirits Company

Northern Utah's only winery, specializing in fruit wines, honey wines, ciders, and brandy

1220 W Jack D Drive, Layton, UT 84041; 801-546-1997
thehivewinery.com

IG Winery

Taste locally blended wine using grapes sourced from Washington, Oregon, California, and Utah

59 W Center Street, Cedar City, UT 84720; 435-TOP-WINE
igwinery.com

Old Town Cellars

OTC wine is blended and bottled on-site using wine sourced from the best wine-growing regions

408 Main Street, Park City, UT 84060; 435-649-3759
otcwines.com

Spanish Valley Vineyards & Winery

Specializing in single-vineyard estate-bottle wines in Moab's Spanish Valley

4710 Zimmerman Lane, Moab, UT 84532; 435-634-1010
moabwinery.com

A vineyard adds to the scenic vista

Kanarra Falls

IN A LANDSCAPE SHAPED BY WATER, it's no surprise there are hundreds of cool waterfalls in Utah. Some streams carved unique slot canyons in southern Utah's sandstone, while others tumble from high alpine snowfields in one of Utah's many mountain ranges. Some of these waterfalls have scenic viewpoints along major highways, while others will require a short hike. Of course, skilled canyoneers have access to many more fantastic waterfalls just out of reach for day hikers. If you are exploring waterfalls in southern Utah, beware of flash floods and keep a close eye on weather conditions upstream.

WATERFALLS

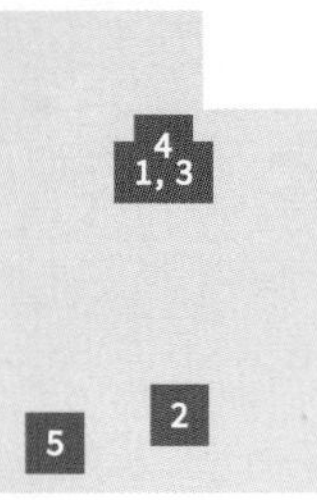

1 Bridal Veil Falls

US 189, Provo Canyon, UT 84604; 801-851-8640
utahcounty.gov/Parks

At more than 600 feet tall, Bridal Veil Falls is one of Utah's highest waterfalls and is often cited as one of the best waterfalls in the United States. Luckily, it's one of the easiest waterfalls to see, as it's located right on US 189 in Provo Canyon. There are several small parking and picnic areas near the base of the falls, including Bridal Veil Falls Park, which is located at the site of a former resort that even had a tram to the top of the falls! Today, you'll have to view the falls from the bottom, but it's a spectacular view, and kids and dogs love splashing in the pool at the bottom of the falls.

2 Calf Creek Falls

Scenic Byway 12 between Escalante and Boulder, UT
utah.com/hiking/calf-creek-falls-lower

If you are driving along Scenic Byway 12 between Escalante and Boulder and want to stretch your legs on a fairly long hike, Calf Creek Falls is a beautiful spot. You will have to choose between Lower Calf Creek Falls and Upper Calf Creek Falls, as they are two different hikes. Lower Calf Creek Falls is the taller and more popular destination, at 126 feet tall. Along the 3-mile trail, you'll pass some granaries and petroglyphs and have plenty of opportunities to cool off in the creek. While Upper Calf Creek Falls is only 2 miles round-trip, it is steep and considerably less crowded than the Lower Falls trail. Both hikes offer a beautiful reward for hiking in the hot desert sun.

3 Cascade Springs

Cascade Scenic Drive between Midway and Sundance, UT

Leaving from the Heber Valley village of Midway, the brand new Cascade Springs highway climbs the Wasatch Mountains for about 30 minutes when you reach the first parking lot for the Cascade Springs. While this isn't a huge waterfall like Bridal Veil Falls, it is impressive in its own way. It's estimated that as much as 7.5 million gallons of water flow from the springs each day! There is an interpretive trail around the springs, mostly on boardwalks over the water. The entire trail consists of three loops and is less than 1 mile in length, so it's an easy hike. Continuing in the same direction, Cascade Springs Road meets up with the Alpine Loop Scenic Byway not far from Stewart Falls and Sundance Mountain Resort. The Cascade Springs Highway is closed in winter; check with the Utah Department of Transportation for latest road conditions.

4 Donut Falls

Big Cottonwood Canyon, Salt Lake City, UT 84121
utah.com/hiking/donUT falls

One of the most popular waterfall hikes near Salt Lake City, this is a great one for the whole family. Located in Big Cottonwood Canyon, the trailhead is less than one hour from either Park City or Salt Lake City in the summer months. There are several parking lots starting at the main highway, so you can make this hike as short as 1.5 miles or longer if you park at the first lot and hike in. There are many great places to stop along the way, and due to the difficulty of the final stretch of the falls, you may prefer to admire them from the bottom. If you are up for some scrambling on slick wet rocks, you'll get to see why they are called Donut Falls, as the water cascades through a donut-shaped hole in the rocks before tumbling down to the creek below.

5 Kanarra Falls

Kanarraville, UT
kanarrafalls.com

Located just south of Cedar City, the trail along the Kanarra Creek marks a stark contrast in the landscapes. Starting in the scrubby high desert and quickly transitioning to one of the red sandstone slot canyons for which Utah is known. Managed by the town of Kanarra, access is limited to 150 people per day. It is highly recommended to purchase tickets online ahead of time, as they sell out on most days. The hike is less than 2 miles each way but considered strenuous in some parts, as there are steep drop-offs and narrow slot canyons. You will be hiking in water for the last half-mile or so, and the water is extremely cold! At the end of the slot canyon, you'll come across several sets of waterfalls, which you can access via ladders and ropes. A new ladder was recently installed at the first falls, but hikers should exercise caution and consider staying below the second waterfall. Even if that sounds daunting, it's worth the hike just to the first waterfall.

6 Mossy Cave Trail

UT 12 between Bryce and Tropic, UT
nps.gov/brca/planyourvisit/mossycave.htm

Traveling east on UT 12 past the main area of Bryce Canyon National Park, you'll see a small parking lot on the right marked "Mossy Cave Trail." In just 1 mile round-trip, you're treated to two natural wonders, all under the shadow of Bryce's famous red rock hoodoos. First, hike to Mossy Cave, which is a cool shelter cave covered in moss and dripping with water. Next, take a side trail to an overlook of a sizable waterfall. You can also hike to the waterfall by walking through the river, starting at the bridge. Up close, this is one of the prettiest waterfalls in Utah because you have a red rock base, white mineral residue, and turquoise pool of water.

Waterfall near Mossy Cave in Bryce Canyon National Park

Provo River Falls

7 Provo River Falls

UT 150 between Kamas and Mirror Lake, UT
utah.com/hiking/provo-canyon-river-waterfalls

As you leave the Wasatch Back for the Uinta Mountains along the Mirror Lake Scenic Highway, this is one of the best places to stop. As you drive towards Mirror Lake, you'll see the falls from the road, and there's a parking lot, restroom, and scenic overlook at the falls. You can also take a short hike to the base of the falls, where several pools offer the perfect spot for a cool splash in the water. Beware of swift water in the summer months, which can pose a danger to small children and dogs. The shaded area around the falls makes a great place for a picnic before continuing the scenic drive to Mirror Lake.

8 Stewart Falls

Sundance Mountain Resort, UT
utah.com/hiking/stewart-falls

Two cascades falling 200 feet make this one of the most popular waterfall hikes in Utah. Located along the Alpine Loop Scenic Byway, there are a few options for reaching the waterfalls. Horseback rides are available from the nearby Sundance Stables, although they book up far in advance. For hikers, you can park at the main trailhead and hike into the falls, which is about a 3.5-mile round-trip hike. From Sundance Resort, you can opt for a slightly shorter hike or take the chairlift to Ray's Summit for an even shorter hike. Expect crowds on this trail, especially on weekends and holidays.

Provo River Fly Fishing

WITH FIVE NATIONAL PARKS, 43 state parks, and topography ranging from red desert canyons to 13,000-foot alpine peaks, most visitors and residents come to Utah for outdoor adventures. While southern Utah is filled with slot canyons and beautiful rock formations, northern Utah is home to the high, snowy peaks, including Kings Peak, Utah's highest point at 13,527 feet. Adventure towns such as Logan, Ogden, Moab, Park City, and St. George make the perfect home base for jumping off on one of these outdoor adventures. It's no wonder that major outdoor retailers have chosen Utah as a home base.

EVEN MORE TO EXPLORE:

Outdoor Adventures

1 Canyoneering

Canyoneering is a super popular sport in Utah. It's a little bit of rock climbing, but also requires hiking, scrambling, rappelling, swimming, and route finding. It's certainly not a sport to be taken lightly, especially during the monsoon months when flash floods are common. Sadly, canyoneers die every summer in flash floods. That said, southern Utah is probably the best place in the country to try canyoneering for the first time. Guiding companies abound, and there are many varieties of slot canyons to suit your skill level.

Buckskin Gulch

Buckskin Gulch is believed to be the longest slot canyon in the world and offers incredible canyoneering opportunities along the Utah-Arizona border.

Grand Staircase Escalante National Monument

This expansive national monument has dozens of slot canyons, from easy hikes to more technically challenging routes.

Zion National Park

The Subway and Virgin River Narrows are some of the most popular canyoneering routes in Zion National Park. Hikers can tackle part of the narrows from the "bottom-up," but you'll need canyoneering skills to complete the full route. Zion Adventure Company in Springdale has guides and gear rental.

2 Dog Sledding

Many Utah visitors are surprised to learn that you can take a dog-sledding tour during the winter months. There are several outfitters in the Park City area that have teams of sled dogs and offer tours, as well as meet-and-greets with the dogs. A sled holds up to two adults and a child, plus the musher. One person rides standing up behind the musher, while the other person rides up front sitting in the sled. Most tours let you switch halfway through, so you can experience both spots. It's such a fun experience to see the dogs and how excited they are to get going. And because it's a fairly passive activity, even little kids can have this great experience.

Bear Ridge Adventures, Coalville

bearridgeadventures.com

Offering 1-hour, 2-hour, and half-day tours with their dogs, this family-owned company has a great team of mushers and dogs.

North Forty Escapes, Oakley

northfortyescapes.com

Offering 1-hour tours in the Uinta Mountains near Park City. Explore wide-open meadows and beautiful Aspen forests.

3 Fly Fishing

While fly fishing is harder than it looks, it's also incredibly rewarding. Utah has a big variety of fishing holes, and it's a year-round sport, even when the flakes are flying. With dozens of designated "Blue River" fishing spots, you're never far from a good fishing hole in Utah. Guiding companies abound, so even if you're just visiting, all you need is a fishing license and some sunscreen, and they will get you suited up for a day on (or in) the water.

Green River

In northeastern Utah, it's estimated that there are 15,000 trout per square mile on the Green River below the Flaming Gorge Dam. That's a lot of fish!

Provo River

My best fishing experience was standing in the Provo River in the shadow of Mount Timpanogos, watching my mom reel in some huge trout! Rocky Mountain Outfitters in Midway offers skilled and caring guides who will almost guarantee you catch something.

Weber River

Another great spot for fly fishing near Salt Lake City is the Weber River, which enters the Great Salt Lake south of Ogden. All Seasons Adventures offers half-day guiding trips with transportation from Park City.

4 Mountain Biking

Utah is often touted as one of the best mountain biking destinations in the world. With the varied terrain, there are biking trails for everyone in Utah. The slick rock trails near Moab are world-famous and draw thousands of cyclists to the Southwest every year. The mountainous regions of Utah are also great for mountain biking. Nearly every ski resort has summer operations that offer mountain biking and chairlift access for cyclists. Park City is the only IMBA certified Gold level mountain biking city in the country. Don't worry if you haven't tried it; there are tons of guiding companies and beginner trails. Many outfitters are now adding e-bikes to their fleets, too!

5 Snowmobiling

Snowmobiling is the perfect outdoor adventure for anyone seeking an adrenaline rush without a huge physical effort. It's also a great way to break up your ski week. Like a jet-ski on the snow, snowmobiles are easy to drive and very beginner-friendly. Most tour companies will even allow children to ride on the back. Utah snowmobile companies offer anything from a 2-hour tour to a multi-day retreat. Wherever you go, you will see blanketed forests of snow, beautiful bare aspen stands, and alpine meadows where you can really open up the engines.

Beaver Creek Lodge, Garden City

beavercreeklodge.com

This lodge near Bear Lake has 11 guest rooms, with overnight packages that include snowmobile rentals. You can rent out the whole lodge, rent a single room, or just swing by for a guided snowmobile tour.

Daniels Summit Lodge, Heber City

danielssummit.com

This snowmobile lodge is in the heart of the Uintas, home of some of Utah's best snow. If you stay overnight in the lodge, cabins, or the private home, you have access to two daily guided snowmobile tours.

North Forty Escapes, Oakley

northfortyescapes.com

Offering 2-hour tours in the Uinta Mountains near Park City. Explore wide-open meadows and beautiful Aspen forests.

6 Snow Tubing

Snow tubing in Utah takes sledding to another level. With dedicated tubing destinations and many ski resorts offering tubing runs in addition to skiing, tubing is great fun for the whole family. As a bonus, most tubing hills have installed magic carpets to haul you uphill, taking out all of the hard work, leaving nothing but fun!

Brian Head, Beaver

brianhead.com

Southern Utah's best ski resort has two tubing hills, one at each base location. There's a 100-foot drop at Giant Steps and a 75-foot drop at the Navajo Tubing Park.

Cherry Peak, Richmond

skicpr.com

For snow tubing at Utah's northernmost ski resort, head to Cherry Peak. Night tubing is extra fun, with music and LED lights adding to the atmosphere of this five-lane tubing hill.

Soldier Hollow, Midway

utaholympiclegacy.org/location/soldier-hollow

Visit the 2002 Olympic venue for cross-country skiing and biathlon, which now also lays claim to the longest tubing lanes in the state. At 1,200 feet, this is not your average tubing hill!

Woodward Park City, Park City

woodwardparkcity.com

With tubing lanes rivaling those at Soldier Hollow, this adventure hub has all kinds of extreme sports, including seven tubing lanes!

7 Utah Olympic Park

3419 Olympic Parkway, Park City, UT; 435-658-4200
utaholympiclegacy.org

The Utah Olympic Park is a must-see for anyone visiting Park City or Salt Lake. This 400-acre venue hosted several events during the 2002 Winter Olympic Games and is still an official U.S. Olympic Committee training site. It has one of only four bobsled/luge tracks in North America, and visitors can experience the thrill themselves on a ride with a professional pilot. In the summer, the whole place turns into an adventure park with extreme tubing down the ski jumps, zip lines, an alpine slide, ropes course, and chairlifts, among other exciting activities. The Flying Ace All-Stars put on a freestyle show on Friday and Saturday evenings in the summer, although you'll often see professional skiers practicing their jumps into the Olympic Freestyle swimming pool at any given time during the day. Lastly, two on-site museums tell the story of the Olympics, as well as the ski history of Utah.

8 Whitewater Rafting

My first multi-day whitewater rafting trip was in Utah, and it remains one of my favorites to this day. Utah has some of the biggest, best, scariest rapids in the nation. We also have some mellow rivers that are great for a family float trip. If you have time for a multi-day trip, you won't regret it! Camping on a sandbar under the dark skies of Utah is an unforgettable experience. OARS Rafting Company has been my whitewater company of choice for every multi-day trip.

Colorado River, Moab

The Colorado River meanders in from Colorado and is pretty mellow in the areas around Moab. There are many opportunities for a float trip near Moab for half a day. For an overnight trip, you can raft from Moab to Lake Powell in about four days.

Green River, Vernal

Floating from the Flaming Gorge dam through Dinosaur National Monument, the Green River is mostly mellow, aside from the infamous Gates of Lodore. There are outfitters offering day trips around Flaming Gorge, or you can choose a 3-to-4-day trip to really soak in the scenery.

San Juan River

In the Four Corners region, the San Juan meanders along the Utah-Colorado border, offering a family-friendly rafting experience. In addition to magnificent scenery, you may also experience some American Indian history, as many ruins and petroglyphs are found here. Single-day and multi-day trips are available.

Weber River

For mellow whitewater rafting in the Salt Lake City area, the Weber River near Ogden has great scenery and Class I and II rapids. Tubing the river is also popular, and it can be a bit of a party scene on the weekends. I recommend families stick to weekday trips! All Seasons Adventures offers 3-hour rafting trips along the river, with transportation from Park City available.

Canyonlands National Park

WHEN IT COMES TO officially accredited Dark Sky Parks and Places, Utah has more than anywhere else in the world. The recent addition of three state parks brings the Utah total to 21. This comes as no surprise to anyone who has spent time in any of Utah's national or state parks. The dark skies here are incredible! With an entire state population of 3.2 million, and 80 percent of those residents living along the Wasatch Front, there is very little light pollution to contend with once you leave the Salt Lake Valley. The month of April was recently designated Dark Sky Month, with fun events planned throughout the state.

EVEN MORE TO EXPLORE:

Dark Sky Parks

Antelope Island State Park
4528 W 1700 S, Syracuse, UT 84075; 801-725-9263
stateparks.utah.gov/parks/antelope-island

Arches National Park
Moab, UT 84532; 435-719-2299
nps.gov/arch

Bryce Canyon National Park
Bryce, UT 84764; 435-834-5322
nps.gov/brca

Canyonlands National Park
Moab, UT 84532; 435-719-2313
nps.gov/cany

Capitol Reef National Park
Torrey, UT 84775; 435-425-3791
nps.gov/care

Cedar Breaks National Monument
UT 143, Brian Head, UT 84719; 435-986-7120
nps.gov/cebr/index.htm

Dead Horse Point State Park
UT 313, Moab, UT 84532; 435-259-2614
stateparks.utah.gov/parks/dead-horse

Dinosaur National Monument
11625 E 1500 S, Jensen, UT 84035; 435-781-7700
nps.gov/dino

East Canyon State Park
5535 S Highway 66, Morgan, UT 84050; 801-829-6866
stateparks.utah.gov/parks/east-canyon

Fremont Indian State Park and Museum
3820 W Clear Creek Canyon Road, Sevier, UT 84766; 435-527-4631
stateparks.utah.gov/parks/fremont-indian

Goblin Valley State Park
Goblin Valley Road, Green River, UT 84525; 435-275-4584
stateparks.utah.gov/parks/goblin-valley

Goosenecks State Park
UT 316 Mexican Hat, UT 84531; 435-678-2238
stateparks.utah.gov/parks/goosenecks

Hovenweep National Monument
Just north and west of Cortez, CO. See website for directions
nps.gov/hove/index.htm

Jordanelle State Park
515 UT 319, Heber City, UT 84032; 435-649-9540
stateparks.utah.gov/parks/jordanelle

Kodachrome Basin State Park
Cannonville, UT 84718; 435-679-8562
stateparks.utah.gov/parks/kodachrome-basin

Natural Bridges National Monument
San Juan County, UT 84533; 435-692-1234
nps.gov/nabr/index.htm

North Fork Park
Middle Bowery Road, Eden, UT 84310; 801-399-8230
webercountyutah.gov/Parks/North_Fork_Park

Rainbow Bridge National Monument
San Juan County, UT; 928-608-6200
nps.gov/rabr

Rockport State Park
9040 UT 302, Peoa, UT 84061; 435-336-2241
stateparks.utah.gov/parks/rockport

Steinaker State Park
8750 N US 191, Vernal, UT 84078; 435-789-4432
stateparks.utah.gov/parks/steinaker

Timpanogos Cave National Monument
2038 Alpine Loop Road, American Fork, UT 84604; 801-756-5239
nps.gov/tica/index.htm

Zion National Park
Springdale, UT 84767; 435-772-3256
nps.gov/zion

Milky way over Zion National Park

Index

N

O

About the Author

Leigh Wilson is an Illinois native from a family of travelers who sparked a severe case of wanderlust that persists to this day. After a 20-year career in buying and marketing, she left the corporate world behind to pursue travel writing. She has lived in Des Moines, Seattle, Chicago, and Tucson, always in search of the next best place to live. In 2020, she moved to Park City, Utah, where she is also a concierge at a luxury ski resort.

Leigh writes about her travels online at CampfiresAndConcierges.com and is a regular contributor to several other travel blogs. She and her Airedale Terrier, Bailey, have spent months on the road exploring the western United States, always in search of the best scenery and tacos!